Special thanks to Evelyn Bergaila, Meg Gannon and Nancy Morgan
for all of their hard work, love and support.

Pages 2–3: Whitehead Institute Splice Garden, Cambridge, Massachusetts

First published in the United Kingdom in 2004 by Thames & Hudson Ltd,
181A High Holborn, London WC1V 7QX

www.thamesandhudson.com

British Library Cataloguing-in-Publication Data
A catalogue record for this book is available from the British Library

ISBN 0-500-51131-4

Printed and bound in China by Imago

[contents]

Introduction by Tim Richardson **6**

Bagel Garden Revisited by Martha Schwartz **20**

Davis Residence, El Paso, Texas **32** Necco Garden, Cambridge, Massachusetts **42** HUD Plaza Improvements, Washington, DC **48**
Limed Parterre with Skywriter, Cambridge, Massachusetts **54** Center for Innovative Technology, Fairfax, Virginia **58**
Turf Parterre Garden, New York City, New York **62** Becton Dickinson, San Jose, California **66** Exchange Square, Manchester, UK **72**

Biographical Essay by Martha Schwartz **80**

US Courthouse Plaza, Minneapolis, Minnesota **88** Whitehead Institute Splice Garden, Cambridge, Massachusetts **94**
Winslow Farms Conservancy, Hammonton, New Jersey **100** Broward County Civic Arena, Fort Lauderdale, Florida **104**
Geraldton Mine Project, Ontario, Canada **108** Bo o1 City of Tomorrow Exhibition, Malmö, Sweden **114**

My Mission by Martha Schwartz **120**

Gifu Kitagata Apartments, Kitagata, Japan **128** Stella Garden, Bala-Cynwyd, Pennsylvania **136**
Miami International Airport Sound Attenuation Wall, Miami, Florida **140** Power Lines, Gelsenkirchen, Germany **144**
King County Jailhouse Garden, Seattle, Washington **148** Spoleto Festival, Charleston, South Carolina **152** Rio Shopping Center, Atlanta, Georgia **158**
Dickenson Residence, Santa Fe, New Mexico **162** The Citadel, City of Commerce, California **166** Jacob Javits Plaza, New York City, New York **170**
Nexus Kashi III Housing Project, Fukuoka, Japan **176** Theme Park East Entry Esplanade, Anaheim, California **182** Paul Lincke Höfe, Berlin, Germany **186**
51 Garden Ornaments, Westphalia, Germany **192** Swiss Re Headquarters, Munich, Germany **198** Lehrter Bahnhof, Berlin, Germany **206**
Doha Corniche, Doha, Qatar **210**

Chronology **216** Bibliography **222** Picture Credits **224**

[Introduction by Tim Richardson]

Martha Schwartz's work is primarily a response to what she perceives as the visual chaos of the world outdoors, a way of superimposing a human sensibility on the unwieldy, unpredictable and mutable medium that is landscape. The exuberant aspects of the Schwartz style – bright color, irreverent humor, unbridled imagination, unusual materials, a limited range of plants, surreal scaling of objects – are a continual source of delight and surprise, and mitigate against the more conventional design values that she displays in her work: rigor, practicality and orderly methodology. But while a sense of fun is an essential facet of Schwartz's work, it should not mask the controlling seriousness of her artistic intention, and the practical basis for her designs.

Unlike other practitioners, Schwartz does not try to manipulate the natural landscape in a subtle way, bending it to her ends by using nature's own palette of trees, shrubs and flowers. For Schwartz, such an approach is lazy or even dishonest, since her argument is that even the notion that unsullied "nature" exists out there is patently false. If that is the case, we can hardly be genuinely inspired by it. In this spirit, Schwartz views any tribute to the abstract majesty of "nature" as hopelessly misplaced, an outmoded and irrelevant homage to the romanticism of the 18th and 19th centuries, or the wilderness fantasies of our own time. Neither does Schwartz rely principally on the power of linear pattern to hint at cosmic awareness, as other garden formalists (from Bramante to Le Nôtre to the Modernists) have done.

8

Instead, Schwartz's unique contribution is to introduce a conceptual or psychic element as the core of her design philosophy: a single idea based on the site's history (human and ecological), its context and its intended use, that is extrapolated to inform every aspect of the design. The result is usually far more complex, symbolically and visually, than this first premise, but the concept nevertheless remains a constant presence – which is why every project in this book has been given a conceptual surtitle. As a visionary artist seeking an honest response to outdoor environments, Schwartz has devised a design vocabulary (literal, visual and symbolic) that is based on what she sees as the needs and aspirations of human beings rather than a vague concept of nature. As a practical landscape architect, this ethos is also a means of making

places useful, meaningful and delightful to people. These artistic and utilitarian aims have always run parallel in her work, but as Schwartz's career has developed they have become more or less indistinguishable.

Where does one place Martha Schwartz? In historical terms, the position she occupies as a formal landscape designer is not unique. Explicit reference to historical design precedent is rare in Schwartz's work, but where she does honor older traditions – notably the parterres of French 17th-century formal gardens, and the ancient Japanese garden tradition – the formalism referred to is founded on a profound relationship and dialogue with nature. Just as the formal tradition in Western garden design since the Renaissance is based on a neo-Platonic appreciation of the potential for pure form in nature (a purity recreated by the formal designer), so Schwartz's use of artificial materials and her conceptual methodology is intended to reveal some profound hidden truths of a place, rather than simply exist as an emulation of nature. Schwartz arrived at her own pioneering version of conceptualism via Modernism – indeed, she still describes herself as a Modernist, and speaks of an abiding admiration for its social dimension, design discipline and functionalism. But only Schwartz's earliest solo work could be described as Modernist – as she gains confidence, the work becomes more exuberant, personal, witty and colorful; the emphasis on purity of line and the abstract passions produced by the arrangement of volumes is usurped by a more humane conceptual narrative.

While Schwartz's rationale is sited comfortably in a historical formalist tradition of landscape, her work is nevertheless out of kilter with the times. As such, she has suffered from the criticism and occasional scorn of her fellow professional landscape architects. If she can sometimes seem combative, a glance at some of the attacks levelled at her will explain why. To some, Schwartz's work is gimmicky, shallow and shoddy. The humor that she includes in her designs is used against her, to demonstrate a supposed lack of integrity or intellectual rigor. She is accused of being aggressive and contrary, or wilfully obscure. But rather than conform to the comfortable lines of contemporary corporate Modernism, or to ally herself with a respectable architectural movement such as Post-Modernism, or to pay lip service to the now fashionable eco-revelatory or "process" design, Schwartz has chosen to remain at the periphery. Schwartz's worst crime is that she is an original.

[The Schwartz Look] The visual component will always dominate first impressions of a landscape design, and Schwartz creates dramatic impact through the use of unexpected, unusual and apparently incongruous elements, which are held within a rigorous formal design.

First, there is color. Schwartz believes that Western society, particularly in its male component, is "color-phobic," and she never shies away from incorporating bright tones – usually vigorously artificial – in her work. This is the aspect of Schwartz's design style that is most consistently vetoed by nervous clients. Schwartz sees color as emotionally evocative, yet capable of playing a valuable role in the creation of a strong sense of imposed order on a site. This is frequently buttressed by the repetition of simple patterns, shapes and motifs which are rendered just as comfortably on a graphic plane (as a gridded parterre or pavement, perhaps) as in three dimensions – say, through lines of living trees. This use of color and serial pattern is particularly useful, Schwartz says, when one is dealing with large, disparate landscape spaces which seem to cry out for a formal unity.

Mutated versions of a familiar landscape and garden elements are often used in Schwartz's work: off-the-shelf materials might be oversized, brightly colored, endlessly repeated, incongruously placed or otherwise altered and misshapen. But these features are never conceived whimsically; the central concept of the piece is always to the fore. New or unusual materials, or original uses for tried and tested ones, are another essential aspect of Schwartz's work – mist machines, brightly painted logs, yellow globes that squirt water, aquarium gravel, colored Plexiglas, stamped concrete forms. Unlikely artifacts might be given a starring role (an idea borrowed from Pop Art): a kitsch frog ornament sprayed with gold paint, an open-bed railway truck, a silk flower, a white sheet fluttering in the wind. On one level they may be startling, puzzling, disarmingly mundane or comic, but these artifacts have a considered role to play in the conceptual scheme.

The sense of deliberate artificiality produced by these means is often allied to an irreverent and sometimes surreal sense of humor. Many of Schwartz's projects will inspire at least a smile, if not a belly laugh, and this is part of the intention. The simplistic view that humor in a design negates or dilutes its fundamental seriousness or importance is anathema to Schwartz, although she is also aware that if the joke is good enough, some people will never penetrate beyond the humor. It is easy to take such comic twists for granted, as they tend to be lightly worn, but few landscape architects are confident enough (or funny enough) to use humor consistently and successfully in their designs. Schwartz is also aware of the close relationship between comedy and anger, and she utilizes a kind of visual sarcasm as a way of venting frustration at, for example, society's sentimental attitude to nature, or a client's parsimony and unrealistic expectations of a project. On a conceptual level, Schwartz's intention is to create a consistently realized narrative that can enrich one's experience of the landscape design in its context. On a material level, the intention is to create an environment that can be enjoyed with no awareness whatsoever of the symbolic scheme that underpins it. A happily balanced coexistence between these twin readings of a single design is difficult to achieve, but Schwartz has been successful because the conceptual level provides an invisible buttress to the material realization. So while the symbolic narrative may have been vital to the designer during the creation of the visual scheme, and ultimately imbues the place with a sense of completeness and

consistency, a symbolic reading is not a necessary adjunct for every visitor. Schwartz believes in the legitimacy of the open interpretation as applied to her designs.

Another benefit of this rigorously conceptual focus is that it paradoxically creates a profound sense of freedom for the artist. For Schwartz, this has been fundamentally the realization that a landscape or garden, essentially an artifact, can be "about" anything – in its intellectual scope, certainly not confined to nature or even the visual world. It was this epiphany that spurred Schwartz's exploitation of landscape as an artistic medium, and the result is that the character of her work is sometimes closer to art installation than landscape architecture.

[The Practicalities] The casual visitor may be delighted and surprised by a Schwartz public space, corporate landscape, art installation or private garden, but a crucial characteristic of these sites is that they have resonance for the people who use them again and again. Most of Schwartz's commissions are for spaces that are intended to be used and enjoyed by a populace or workforce – at lunchtime, as a resting place during shopping, as a spot to rendezvous with friends, or as a place for a coffee break. Schwartz often remarks that the ultimate test of a design's success is whether or not the space is actually used. For this designer, all public art carries with it a set of obligations that are not to be found in the museum or gallery space. So beneath the exuberant exposition of the designer's imaginings, there lies a practical strategy based on problem-solving. Schwartz does not have a wild idea and then try to fit it around the needs of the space: the conceptual idea for the piece comes as a result of on-the-ground site visits, research, client input and the practical needs of the people who are to use the place.

In this context, the practical problem of seating is as relevant to Schwartz as her own artistic integrity and its formal expression. Even the most astonishing Schwartz designs will contain comfortable places to sit, either singly or in groups, in sun or shade, in private seclusion or in a spot where it is possible to people-watch surreptitiously. Through seating, the ancient role of landscape as a place for escape and contemplation can be honored in an urban environment. Again and again in Schwartz's designs, the role of benches and other forms of seating are central to the layout. Schwartz is also alive to the importance of the psychology of people who use public spaces. For example, there are times when a person may just want to hang around for a few minutes rather than commit themselves formally to the space by sitting down, so at the fringes of her designs Schwartz likes to include places (not seats) where it is possible to perch or lean. Many of the seating layouts in Schwartz's designs maintain this delicate balance of private space in the public or semi-public domain.

Traffic management is another unglamorous but essential facet of Schwartz's designs. Many plazas are adjacent to streets or even have roadways traversing them, so Schwartz's design vocabulary has been expanded to describe a range of street furniture necessary for vehicular management. Wherever possible, Schwartz will customize or design her own bollards, cross-walks and other utilitarian devices, so that everything visible in the space contributes to its designed integrity. And it is not just automobiles that need direction in a landscape design: another practical preoccupation for Schwartz is wayfinding and orientation for pedestrians. The bright colors, unusual structures and bold patterning in these designs often play a role in pointing the way, particularly in large open spaces or inside office buildings.

Perhaps the biggest practical challenge for any landscape architect is forging a relationship with clients. Every designer has problems in this area, but in the case of Martha Schwartz, the challenging nature of the work has created particular difficulties and frustrations. Schwartz is often exasperated to arrive at a site immediately after a landmark building has been constructed, to find that very little or no money has been earmarked for the treatment of the landscape or open spaces. In some cases, the funds needed for building or maintaining the simplest living green space have not been factored into the budget, so a design made entirely of inanimate matter must be constructed. A client who has commissioned an avant-garde office building might have only the vaguest, most conservative notions of the type of landscape that might be built round it – generally a variation on the "something green would be nice" theme. Then, once Schwartz's design has been accepted, it is common for clients subsequently to attempt to water down or eliminate the proposals, particularly if there has been a change of personnel at the top of the organization. A few months on, that steel-fabric cloud-fountain or those blue-steel palm trees do not seem such a good idea. Schwartz is faced with refiguring the design or walking out, and it is to the practice's credit that it rarely resorts to the latter. One of Schwartz's strengths is an ability to replan aspects of a design without compromising its integrity.

Schwartz's style has changed since her time during the 1980s in partnership with her then husband, landscape architect Peter Walker. The work of that office, which is distinguished by a linear formalism and manipulation of space reminiscent of Le Nôtre, certainly informed Schwartz's earlier solo work, which is often preoccupied with geometry and formal axes on a graphic plane. Her earlier training as a printmaker consolidated this graphic methodology, and she has never lost the Modernistic dependence on subtraction as a guiding principle. However, it was her artistic background which led Schwartz away from Modernism and into the wilder shores of landscape design, as she came to see that an idea could be realized graphically, sculpturally, literally and symbolically – all at the same time. Schwartz has found a comfortable professional place midway between visual artist and landscape architect, and is the leading light of a tiny group of conceptualist landscape designers now practicing that includes Topher Delaney in San Francisco, Ken Smith in New York (who worked closely with Schwartz for several years) and Claude Cormier in Montreal. Despite the inherent conservatism of most public bodies and corporations, the populist appeal, practicality, economy and originality of the conceptual approach is becoming more widely accepted, and commissions for these practitioners have been received from some unexpected quarters. Perhaps Schwartz's greatest influence on the visible landscape scene – and particularly in the sphere of garden design, even though relatively few of her gardens have been realized – has been the enthusiasm for unusual or artificial materials which she has pioneered; the use of Astroturf, initially scandalous and now widespread, is a good example. Meanwhile, Schwartz continues to demonstrate not just that a landscape can be made of anything, but also that it can be about anything.

[Bagel Garden Revisited by Martha Schwartz]

Completed over twenty years ago, the Bagel Garden was probably the apex of my career, something that has been difficult for me to accept given that this was the first landscape I ever made. I doubt now that I will ever make a landscape that is more important than the Bagel Garden. For many years I avoided lecturing about it because I did not want to be branded by a single project. Because of its small scale and temporary nature, it seemed a trivial work on which to base a career. I was afraid of becoming "The Bagel Lady" and the words "creator of the Bagel Garden" appearing on my headstone.

At the beginning of my career, I truly believed that I would generate work with more importance, depth and daring than what the Bagel Garden turned out to be. When I made it, the garden seemed a baby-step, a sketch, a small, humble work, but I now realize that this little project was a powerful and lucky first-step into the profession. It kickstarted my career, established me as a presence in the profession and created a mark in the sand that eventually defined the beginning of the post-modern era in landscape architecture. I wish I could claim these were my intentions for the garden, but, quite frankly, my primary objective was to provide amusement by playing a practical joke on my then-husband, Peter Walker.

At the time I had been working in nearby Newton, apprenticing with Bill Pressley. Although I enjoyed the people in the office, the work we produced was far from the art I hoped to make. I was bored and frustrated at the discrepancy between my goals as an artist and what it appeared I would be doing as a landscape architect. The remaking of our frontyard therefore became an increasingly beguiling opportunity to create a project and to keep my hands and imagination busy. I had never done an installation before, and in the 1980s installation art was not yet a common art practice. I would have to pay for it myself and had little money; worse, I would have to negotiate

with Pete over who had artistic rights to design the garden. Still, the mere prospect of making something myself and scheming about the garden made me happy.

I decided to avoid a confrontation over the design of our frontyard by waiting for Pete to go away on a business trip. And although I had set up a bagel-dipping production line in the attic of the townhouse a few weeks prior to his departure, Pete never discovered it. When he left for his trip in the spring of 1979, I quickly installed the garden so that it would be in place upon his return. I thought it would be a funny coming-home stunt, and since the materials were placed temporarily within the existing boxwood hedges, there would be no harm done.

Returning home, Pete was greeted by a handful of friends I had invited over for a "lawn party." We were a bit tipsy and just hanging out on the brick sidewalk (which substituted for a lawn in this case) gazing into the newly installed Bagel Garden while genteelly sipping our mint juleps. I had invited Alan Ward, one of my classmates from Harvard's Graduate School of Design and a talented photographer, to come to the party and asked him to take record shots of the installation. He showed up with his large-format camera.

Marie Brenner, a writer for *New York Magazine* who was living in our house that summer, encouraged me to send Alan's photographs to *Landscape Architecture* magazine. It had never occurred to me to do this, given the intention and nature of the installation. But Alan's photographs had transformed the garden into beautiful and rich images of amazing color and detail. The photographs were remarkable in themselves, and I decided to send them to the magazine, not expecting any response.

Grady Clay, the editor of *Landscape Architecture*, wrote back that he was interested in publishing the Bagel Garden and asked me to write an article about it. I immediately went to work doing a drawing (which ended up being a spoof on working drawings, showing details of a bagel and how to place each one in the garden) and wrote the piece. The article was essentially a critique of the artistic malaise it seemed to me the profession was in at the time and reflected my dissatisfaction with what was being produced by the large corporate offices. I simply made the case that a bagel could be an "appropriate" landscape material (appropriateness was a big thing at the time in the practice): it was cheap, anybody could install it, it was a "democratic material," did well in the shade, did not need watering and so on. The piece was published a few months later.

In a further strange twist in the history of the Bagel Garden, Grady decided to put Alan's photograph on the magazine's front cover. This was an incredibly bold decision for its foresight and riskiness, for which Grady would later suffer the consequences, as many subscriptions were cancelled by angry landscape architects who felt that the garden was below the dignity of the profession. The Bagel Garden also put Grady at odds with the majority of the American Society of Landscape Architects (which publishes the magazine), and he eventually lost his position as editor-in-chief. I had mixed feelings, then, about the fact that the publication of the Bagel Garden had transformed me from a complete unknown into a cover girl. It was my fifteen minutes of fame.

In the following issue of *Landscape Architecture* magazine, the otherwise usually limp editorial section "Cuts and Fills" (the whole northern hemisphere might have been redesigned and it would only invoke two or three letters) was entirely devoted to letters in response to the Bagel Garden, pro and con. The garden generated a heated debate over its seriousness, importance, relevance and meaning. Some people felt that the garden was evidence of how the profession itself had gone astray; it was evil incarnate. After two decades of trying to recast landscape architecture as a serious, science-based profession, the article and the magazine's brazen publication of it was seen as a slap in the face to many practitioners who felt that I and the magazine were trivializing and debasing the profession. Others argued that the garden was a great breath of fresh air and that the profession could stand some scrutiny. The funniest critique was that I was "only in it for the money" (it transpires that this "ploy" was *not* in fact a viable get-rich-quick-scheme). I'm sure many people hoped that I would fade away and never be heard of again.

The success – or notoriety – I gained as a result of this publicity taught me many lessons, and the garden's promotion set the course for my future work. With the benefit of hindsight, I've realized that the single smartest and most important professional decision I've made was to ask Alan Ward to photograph the installation. Without knowing it beforehand, I sensed that this was an event – a "happening," in the parlance of the day – and that it would only exist in reality for a very short time. My photography studies in art school had taught me the power of an image, and I believed in photography as its own art-form. It is largely through Alan's artistry that the Bagel Garden has existed as an image and an idea.

The Bagel Garden popped up at the beginning of the media's ascent and our entry into the information age. It was the first time a work of landscape design had been propelled into stardom (or infamy) almost entirely through the power of an image and the media. The garden marked the beginnings of landscape architecture's rise in visibility, and I believe it spurred many young designers to think of landscape architecture as an exciting field of design. Although many argue that media exposure is not a valid means of judging landscape architecture (architecture doesn't seem to have a problem with it), it is largely through the media that the design professions have flourished. The image has proved to be a powerful vehicle for the transmission of ideas and information. Most of us have only experienced landscapes through images, which, though not as good as being there in person, is better than not experiencing them at all.

The photographs by Alan Ward were the defining moment of the garden, without which this little installation would never have come to light. They illustrate the beauty of the greens and purples of the existing maple and the colored gravel, creating a very somber, serious mood for the silly bagels.

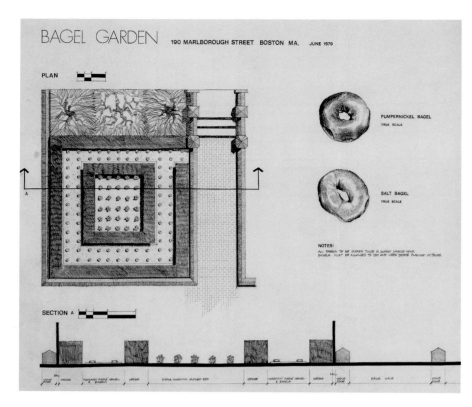

A plan and section drawing spoofing the standard working drawing conventions. They carefully illustrate and measure out how one puts bagels into the garden.

Cover of *Landscape Architecture* magazine, January 1980, as conceived of by the then editor, Grady Clay. Grady's clever use of this little garden created the ruckus.

30

The garden was retro-fitted into the existing system of host gardens in Back Bay, Boston. The boxwood hedges and maple tree were already in place.

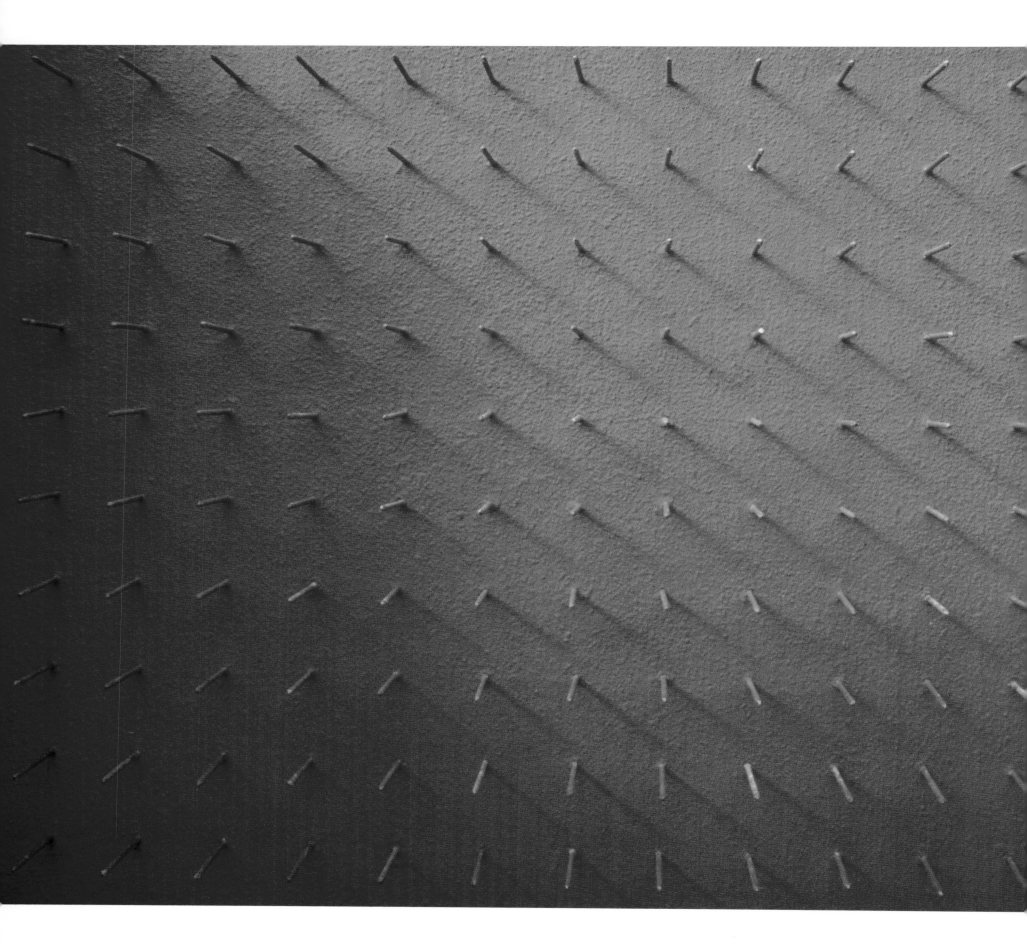

interlocking **boxes** contain spikes, heaps, shards and shelves

Davis Residence

El Paso, Texas   1996
Client: Sam Davis

A series of six vibrantly colored and roofless garden rooms occupies an enclosed, rectangular 37-by-60-feet (11-by-18-meters) space in a portion of a garden in El Paso. The owners, Anne and Sam Davis, had spent the previous 25 years working on an English-style garden, inspired by Sissinghurst but utilizing a palette of desert plants. Anne Davis then decided to offset this traditional garden with a Schwartz creation in an unprepossessing rectangle of space between the garage and garden. Schwartz describes the brief: "Anne said, 'You can do whatever you want as long as it stays inside the box.'"

Thinking outside the box, Schwartz came up with this take on the traditional Mexican garden, with visual echoes of sunny courtyards seen through small, square, cut-out windows, colored walls and beds of cacti. She acknowledges the obvious influence of Luis Barragán, and also the roofless outdoor-room spaces constructed by minimalist artist Donald Judd at Marfa, Texas. But the basic concept was based on the idea of containment: "The box was so strong an underlying element that it couldn't be ignored," Schwartz says. "I tried to integrate the box – the original

four walls – with other boxes within. That made the original, ugly walls disappear."

Each of the rooms contains a different symbolic statement in stone, metal or cactus plants. A terrifying grid of 12-inch spikes sticking out from the walls of one room is a reference to the barbed wire at the nearby border with Mexico; a sculpted cone of gravel visually echoes the Rockies or local industrial slagheaps; a line of blue-glass shards atop one wall refers to the popular urban burglar deterrent; a row of phallic cacti towers – imperiously, menacingly, humorously – occupies the mirrored space designated as a changing room for the adjacent swimming pool.

Schwartz says that the garden was conceived less as a homage to Mexico than in the spirit of an 18th-century English folly – "a toy or a plaything placed in the middle of a naturalistic setting" – a comparison which the owners enjoy. "Today," says Schwartz, "things that have happened inside the box have jumped out and are now in the rest of the garden – structural echoes, like a new stucco wall. The Davises now have an integrated garden."

A computer-generated illustration [above], one of the earliest in the office by Rick Casteel, that showed a linear pool to replace the existing amoeba-shaped pool.

View [right] of the six boxes or rooms from the pool area. The broken glass shards protect the most private room – the bathroom.

View of the boxes/rooms from the pool [below] and of the garden from the existing "English Garden" [bottom].

Inside this room is an ominous wall of nails. Schwartz explains that along with the Davis's wish to use cacti, this room itself is an architectural cactus. It can also be used to hang up clothes and wet bathing suits and towels.

The middle room in the iconic "heart" of the composition. It is a pile of granite stone-pieces of the substrate that underlies this region. The form of the pile pays tribute to the surrounding mountains. The walls are painted gold to suggest something holy or precious.

Hallways are an important part of the composition and suggest a maze-type garden. Small plazas further confuse what is inside, outside, public or private.

On the top of a wall in a long, narrow space
Schwartz placed rough-hewn glass crystals,
which have an intriguing dual function. On the
one hand, the shards give protection against
intruders; on the other, the bluish glass refracts
light onto the white walls for the visitor's
contemplation and delight.

The Saguaro Cactus Room is the room of spirituality, as this cactus is believed by the Native Americans to contain human spirits.

This is the changing room where you can dress and undress in front of a mirror-covered wall. The square bullet-hole windows are aligned so that you can see straight through to the neighbor's garden.

the purity of **math** expressed through Necco wafers

Necco Garden

Cambridge, Massachusetts   1980
Client: Massachusetts Institute of Technology

A temporary (day-long) installation commemorating May Day comprised a geometric pattern made up entirely of Necco wafers (a classic American sweet) donated by the New England Candy Company, who manufacture them at premises nearby. However, the confectionery had no symbolic role: "This piece was dealing with geometries and a clash of axes," Schwartz explains. "It was not so much a social commentary."

One grid sat comfortably within the formal boundaries of MIT's Killian Court, the other axis related to a new Michael Heizer piece that had recently been sited towards the edge of the courtyard. The historical reference – one which recurs in Schwartz's work – was the 17th-century French formal garden, in that space is organized by patterning the horizontal ground-plane, by using objects in a serial fashion, and through the use of parallel lines to exaggerate distances. The mathematical subject matter reflected the research role of MIT, while the design resonated with the architectural grandeur and formality of the Great Court, as well as relating to the larger urban context of the grid of Back Bay Boston, visible across the Charles River.

Used and flat tires were collected from the streets over a period of weeks. They were then spray painted to match the exact colors of the Neccos. It was discovered that they needed to be undercoated first with white paint.

Nancy Dilland carefully places Necco wafer candies along guideline strings [left]. Chocolate- and licorice-flavored wafers were eliminated because the dark colors (brown and black) did not read well against the grass.

While the larger scale of the tires held the geometry of the space well, the smaller scaled Neccos fought with the grass, creating bumpy lines that were not as successful as the tires. Schwartz maintains that temporary installations such as this are an excellent way to experiment and learn.

The garden an hour before completion and the start of the Ultimate
Frisbee tournament planned to take place in the Necco Garden.

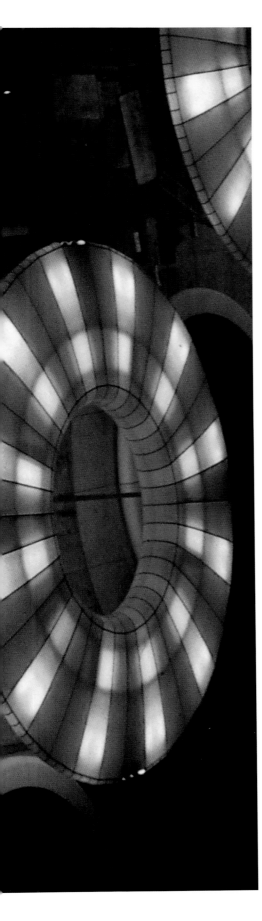

circles in the air and on the ground

HUD Plaza Improvements
Washington, DC   1998
Client: US General Services Administration

Although Marcel Breuer's 1968 building for the Department of Housing and Urban Development (HUD) in Washington, DC bears a richly textured facade, its 6-acre (2.4-hectare) plaza was without trees or public amenities. The plaza was designed to showcase the building, but was virtually unusable by HUD's 4,800 employees and was considered to have created a negative image for the department. Adding to the desolation of this landscape was the fact that the base of the building is a solid wall of dark stone that prohibits a visual connection between the life of the building within and that without. HUD's objective for the plaza was to reactivate it by commissioning a new design that would also express the agency's mission of creating habitable spaces for people.

Following a two-year public process, a scheme featuring a "floating garden" of repeated circular forms was realized. This theme recalled Breuer's own use of geometric designs for screens, walls, and ceilings. "Breuer loomed large," Schwartz says. "We did research on his work and came up with the concept of using circles; he loved circular motifs. At the Whitney Museum, for example, he used circular lights. He also liked pure form, and we thought the circle would resonate with Breuer's architecture. Then we chose colors using the primer Breuer had devised: cobalt blue, vermilion, a bright orangey yellow. Finally, I wanted the expression of the installation to be very, very light – almost floating, in contrast to the 'modern Brutalism' of the building's massiveness above the wedge-shaped pilotis."

The plaza is transformed through a strong ground plane patterning, a series of concrete planters containing grass, and the ring-shaped canopies. The 30-feet (9-meters) diameter planters – which Schwartz calls "grass cookies" – double as seating and seem to float off the ground. The canopies, fabricated of vinyl-coated plastic fabric, are raised 14 feet (4.3 meters) above the ground plane on steel poles. As this plaza is built over an underground garage, the canopies also provide shade and visual protection from the offices above on a plaza that was not designed to support the soil required for trees. These "floating" elements help preserve the original relationship between the plaza and the pilotis of the Breuer building.

The original plan for colored canopies was rejected by a new HUD Secretary after the project had started – which almost led to a lawsuit. As a compromise, they were realized in pure white instead of the original Breuer color palette. "We're in a culture that's color-phobic," says Schwartz. "The new Secretary was afraid of the attention the color may have attracted. He was afraid it might not be dignified or could appear frivolous. I don't think a woman would have had that reaction. The new color scheme makes it a different kind of plaza: it's more contained, cooler, more federal. Very Washington, DC. I would have preferred it as it had been originally conceived, but I like it white, too – it gives a fresher appearance to the area."

Lighting enhances the identity of the plaza. Lit from within, the canopies glow at night, recalling the lanterns that illuminate paths in Japanese gardens. A fiber-optic tube casts colored light under the planters, making them appear to float on a cloud of light. For the dark wall at the base of the building, a backlit photo mural was planned as safety lighting. It was to have reflected the people and faces of HUD, creating a dramatic backdrop for the plaza. The murals were eliminated because it was feared they would give the appearance of spending money at a time when the agency itself was under scrutiny. The cost of the project was equivalent to that of simply replacing the original slate pavers.

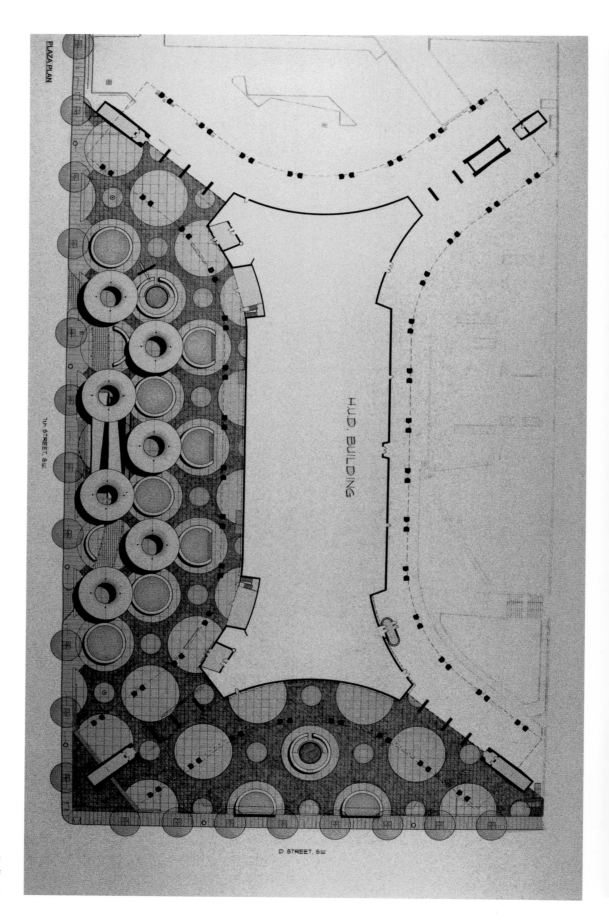

PLAZA PLAN

7th STREET, SW

H.U.D. BUILDING

D STREET, SW

Plan of the south and north plazas illustrating the
idea of a floating garden of circles – a motif
"approved" by the building's architect, Marcel Breuer.

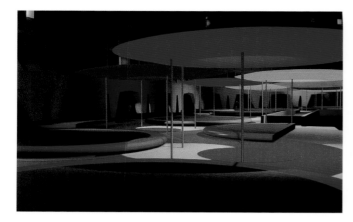

An illustration of the original scheme for the plaza [above]. The use of color was requested by the then-director of HUD, Henry Cisneros, to reflect the ethnic diversity of the workers within the building. Color was eliminated by Andrew Cuomo, the subsequent director.

Under the canopies [left], the material of which is a standard, off-the-shelf, vinyl plastic used on commercial awnings. The vinyl fabric has great translucency, allowing the disks to glow like "Lifesavers" at night [below]; 3ft (0.9m) wide, precast concrete edges provide seating around the glass circles [bottom].

straight lines intended to **heal** a blighted space

Limed Parterre With Skywriter

Cambridge, Massachusetts   1988
Client: Office for the Arts at Harvard and Radcliffe

Harvard University commissioned a public-art piece to mark the restoration of the quadrangle of Moors Hall, a neo-classical dormitory or hall-of-residence. However, the one-day installation made by Martha Schwartz was not a celebration but a critique of the university's building work.

"That piece was a gesture of healing," she explains. "What we were trying to heal was the damage that had been done by the addition of a new luncheon room in the basement of the building. To stop it being subterranean, they dug down into the lawn of the quadrangle and made a ramp so that people in the cafeteria had daylight. It absolutely defaced the landscape amid those buildings. And there was no one there to defend it – no one in the university thought this was important."

To restore the relationship between building and quadrangle, and to emphasize how important the flatness of the space had previously been, six "pilasters" were painted by hand down the facade of Moors Hall, onto the cafeteria addition, and then across the length of the lawn. Schwartz describes this gesture as "a big band-aid." There was an airshow that day, and the intention (unrealized) was to mirror the quadrangle stripes with a "skywriter" of six jetstreams at 5,000 feet, ultimately converging at the horizon.

The pilasters of the building were drawn across the top of the new cafeteria addition, down its facade and onto the green lawn. Schwartz calls this a great band-aid to repair the relationship between the lawn and the historic building, a composition that was destroyed by the new construction.

Artist Ross Miller added another level to the Parterre [below] by building weirdly configured picnic tables to suggest an array of different possibilities in social interaction. Schwartz drew the lines on top of Miller's table as an interaction point between the two installations.

a flat landscape of linear **pattern**

Center for Innovative Technology

Fairfax, Virginia 1988
Client: Center for Innovative Technology

"This was the first job ever given to me by an architect – the first time I was asked to do something real," Schwartz recalls. The graphic basis for this rooftop design reflects the more conventionally Modernist tone of Schwartz's earlier work in conjunction with Peter Walker. "It was a simple project that was all about patterning. Over time, I became more confident sculpturally," she says.

A flat landscape of linear patterning includes gravel strips alternating with meadow grass, a grid of gazing balls under a linden bosk or smallwood, and a dining patio. Gently curved on one side, the bosk is planted in plum-colored crushed gravel with stripes of loose-set stones that create the impression of garden paths. Within the bosk, rows of blue mirror globes appear as pieces of the building's mirrored facade and recall flowers in bloom beneath the trees. Randomly placed gold and grey concrete blocks form a parallelogram-shaped plaza that echoes the shape of the site's tower building. Near the cafeteria, a concrete checkerboard of light and dark pavers forms a dining patio.

"This is where I started learning," Schwartz says. "There were very few areas to plant trees on. The idea was that we took the motif of this crazy building – like an upside-down pyramid with a series of colored-glass areas – and we worked with that idea on the ground plane. But we had a real battle with the client. It was interesting – they had commissioned this wild building, but they were so conservative with the landscape."

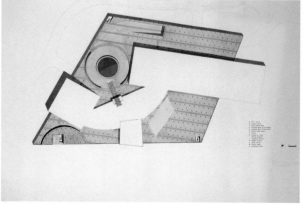

The original plan [left] had the buildings, which are on top
of a parking structure, sitting in a striated field of tall grasses. This
scheme was made unfeasible due to the available depth of soil.
Lawn and gravel were used instead.

The blue gazing globes were installed long after completion due to the clients' fear of them being too radical. The fact that they could not be used as something else (such as lighting or seating) was also a problem. Schwartz set out a line of temporary globes until the client became comfortable with the idea. The remaining globes were then installed.

the **horizontal** overcomes the vertical

Turf Parterre Garden

New York City, New York   1988
"New Urban Landscape" exhibition; sponsor: Olympia and York

One of Schwartz's most successful installations, the Turf Parterre Garden, was conceived as part of "The New Urban Landscape," an exhibition of work by 30 different artists and architects marking the completion of the World Financial Center complex in Lower Manhattan.

The facade of the World Financial Center, designed by architect Cesar Pelli, is distinguished by a grid pattern of square windows and granite. The intent of the Turf Parterre Garden was to take the architect's facade pattern and reapply it to the building, creating another layer in the form of a garden. Squares of turf were removed from the lawn, creating a mirror of the building's facade. The pattern continued, misregistered, up the facade of the building in the form of artificial turf squares adhered to its surface.

"The topic here was the urban landscape," says Schwartz. "Battery Park City is essentially a suburban development – complete with the requisite portion of green lawn – spliced onto Lower Manhattan. It is totally meaningless in that context. There is no distinction between the ground plane and the facade of the building because the ground plane is meaningless. Pelli's idea was to enclose those buildings in a wallpaper of serial fenestration. My idea was to wallpaper his wallpaper by tearing off a piece of the romantic landscape and reapplying it to the building."

The Turf Parterre Garden and Schwartz's reaction to the site is emblematic of her attitude towards more naturalistic modes of landscape design. "I don't like to do naturalism because I feel it's a fake. It's a pastiche, it's sentimental, avoiding the issue of our occupying and building the landscape. Naturalism is a way of avoiding that truth. I also feel it is a historical style, and I don't understand why you would go back and copy a style of 100 years ago. It doesn't seem an honest approach – the honest thing is to grapple with the world as it is today. Naturalism is a balm, this idea that real nature is all around us. It's seen almost as a token tithe to the environment – but it's meaningless."

The parterre was conceived as a piece of landscape wallpaper applied to the architectural wallpapering of the buildings. It was, as Schwartz puts it, wallpapering wallpaper.

Schwartz's intention was to make it appear as if pieces of turf had been cut out, lifted off the earth, and exported on to the facade of the building.

serial evolution of a **line**

Becton Dickinson

San Jose, California 1990
Client: Becton Dickinson Immunocytrometry Division

In this project, there is no metaphorical relationship between the landscape design and the characteristics of the institution, a medical research center, although Schwartz's theoretical methodology was appropriate, given the nature of the work at the establishment. "I wanted to express the concept of the line," Schwartz says. "It's almost a mathematical, serial piece. It's a simple equation, but when it is actually applied, it does funny things."

The area to be redesigned occupied a long, narrow, glazed space between large buildings, used as an informal area for meetings and breaks. Twelve garden rooms, enclosed by white trellis planted with ficus to create hedge-seats, are graduated in size from one end of the passage to the other. The smallest space is just 4-feet (1.2-meters) square and 6 inches (15 centimeters) high; the largest is 24-feet (7.3-meters) square with a 16-feet (4.9-meters) hedge. The smaller rooms provide seating for the adjacent cafeteria. The larger rooms are more secluded meeting spaces, and contain painted-concrete reflecting pools with spiky sansevieria specimens. Placed on the tiled surrounds, which double as seats, are yellow globes that squirt water.

A fishtail palm colonnade reinforces the atrium's central axis. The atrium's concrete floor is composed of poured concrete painted in green and black stripes, and this pattern extends beyond the building to organize the motor court, where a spiral rock and ficus dome serves as a focal point.

A tilted spiral hedge and rock mound form a turn-around
at the entrance to the Becton Dickinson building.

Wood-slatted boxes form the trellis-like structure and the support for a winding hedge. Small vines, almost invisible in these photographs, have covered the white trellises to form a green wall.

On this serial progression piece, the "hedge" goes
from large, tall rooms (meeting rooms) to small,
low rooms (at the cafeteria). At this end the
orange island, planted with Mother-in-Law's-
Tongue (*Sansevieria trifasciata*), gets spat out
of the system.

a great **curve** enfolds a city space

Exchange Square
Manchester, UK 2000
Client: Manchester Millennium

Plazas are known as squares in England, but this city-center space is anything but square – a sloping, approximately triangular site sandwiched between shops, offices, the Corn Exchange, a road and an ancient pub. The 1996 IRA bomb blast on Manchester city center provided the impetus for this regeneration: the new square marks the boundary between the city's ancient cathedral precincts and a brand-new shopping quarter: a large Marks & Spencer store takes up one side of the square.

"It was like gluing two pieces of the city together," Schwartz says. "The upper part by the modern quarter is cooler, with concrete, steel and granite. The lower section, on the cathedral side, is made up of yellow puddingstone [Yorkstone]." The main practical consideration was the sloping site, which generated the major structural element, a series of curving pathways or ramps, which gently arc down and across the space, divided by low walls that also act as informal seats. The effect is of a gently curving amphitheater, satisfying to traverse and an attractive place to linger. As Schwartz says, "In general, successful public places allow people to get together and sit, to hang out informally, in groups or individually. People want choices, and a space should be designed to accommodate a wide range of uses – formal and informal, organized and spontaneous. It should encourage traditional activities and inspire new uses. The space should be a backdrop for people when in use and provide a foreground when not in use. You can't get any more prescriptive than that."

There is a conventional stairway at the top end of the ramps that directly connects the upper "shopping" portion of the site to the lower Cathedral district. Running the width of the square where the steps emerge below is a stylized dry riverbed of cracked rocks, punctuated by low bubbling fountains and lined with river birch. This feature follows the line of Manchester's medieval Hanging Ditch, an ancient boundary, and it has become a popular "stepping stone" game for children.

The upper part of the square is paved in granite and provides more seating areas in the unlikely form of large-wheeled, open-bed, blue railway trucks, spaced along stylized "tracks" – a reference to the city's role in the Industrial Revolution, not least as a transport hub. These trucks were originally intended to be movable – placed on real tracks – but this facet of the design and, more controversially, Schwartz's plans for perspex blocks containing artifacts found on site during construction and a gateway marked by a grove of 30-feet (9-meters) high, blue-metal palm trees, were shelved by the city authorities.

Those decisions compromised the design to a degree, but Martha Schwartz, Inc. pursued its policy of perseverance and compromise where necessary. Crucially, the revised scheme did not negate any of Schwartz's own criteria for a public space: "It should be attractive enough to make people curious about it. It should have an 'up' feeling about it. It should not have to be occupied to look good, nor should it place undue focus on privacy – people like to look at each other, without being obvious about it.

"No one wants to be the first to sit down in an open space, so that problem must be addressed. There is also a pleasure in being able to sit down on things that do not look as if they are meant to be sat on – people often like to perch. They like choices in terms of where they sit, and whether or not to be in the shade or face the sun. It's about people, fundamentally. A space is successful if people use it. Communities, cities and, most importantly, individuals derive their self-image as citizens from these public places."

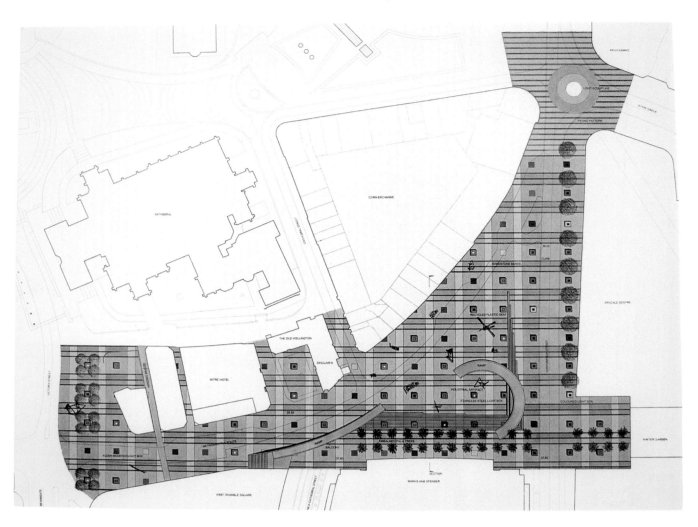

74

One of two plans submitted as part of a competition [above]. This plan, which was not selected, showed a scheme based upon a different grading concept that had the main space of the square below the department store and at the same level of the Corn Exchange. The winning scheme had the main design at the level of the department store.

As part of this scheme, industrial artifacts were included as sculpture [below and right].

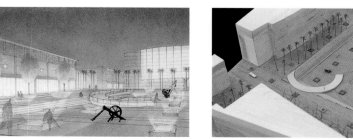

Kids come to play with and in the new
Hanging Ditch.

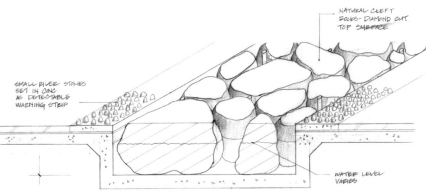

NATURAL CLEFT
ROCKS - DIAMOND CUT
TOP SURFACE

SMALL RIVER STONES
SET IN CONC
AS DETECTABLE
WARNING STRIP

WATER LEVEL
VARIES

SCALE 1:10

The source of the Hanging Ditch was designed to look as though the underground pipes that had captured the ancient water course, had been pulled up out of the earth to allow the water to flow once more.

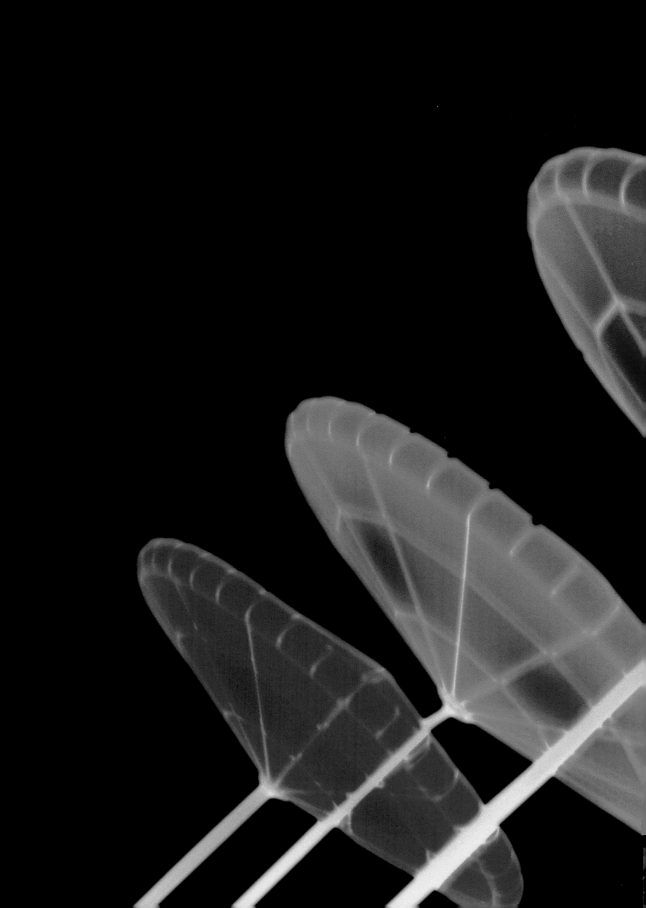

[Biographical essay by Martha Schwartz]

I come from a right-brained background, a characteristic which has run through my family for generations. Both of my great grandfathers, who came to this country from Russia and Romania at the turn of the twentieth century, were tailors. Their grandchildren (my parent's generation) were the first generation to have access to university, and several used their education to move from tailoring to architecture; my father, sister, uncle, cousin and son are architects. My husband is an architect, and many of my closest friends are architects. The rest of my family are an assortment of graphic designers, painters and engineers – with a few psychologists thrown into the mix.

As a young man, my father, Milton Schwartz, had taught under Louis Kahn at the University of Pennsylvania, later going on to establish a large office and designing high-rise housing projects. I grew up playing with dried-out magic markers on the floor of my father's office. The broken toilet templates I was given to play with and the *Sweet's Catalogue* (particularly the details of door and window jambs) almost completely dissuaded me from ever becoming an architect. Having early intimate experience with architectural practice, with its attention to detail and the protracted timeline of building projects, I didn't feel I had the temperament to be an architect. As much as I liked looking at buildings and was schlepped from pillar to post on family "field trips," I grew aware as a little girl that I needed a loose, less structured arena. In short, I needed to become an artist.

Growing up in Philadelphia allowed me to spend every Saturday morning in the basement of the Philadelphia Art Museum taking children's art courses, my preferred activity being to leave classes early and wander into the interiors installations. My favorite by far was the Japanese tea house, where we kids hung out until our mothers came to pick us up. The softly lit room and the magic of the tea house in its garden setting, curiously situated within the bowels of the museum, induced a calm, trance-like feeling that drew us in every weekend. There were other such fantasy-spaces I loved as a child: the greenhouse environments at Longwood Gardens, on the Dupont Estate, south-east of Philadelphia. The great greenhouses were like giant formal living rooms made from such natural materials as grass, flowers and hedges. The ambiguity

of indoor and outdoor space was full of wonder for me. I fantasized about living in a house, with my bed set out on a huge carpet of lawn that would allow me to step upon fresh grass first thing in the morning. The idea of living in an environment made out of nature still intrigues me. It's why I love gardens, the very spaces where civilization meets nature.

I enrolled as an art student at the School of Architecture and Design at the University of Michigan and majored in printmaking. During school I paid close attention to the earthworks artists, such as Robert Smithson, Walter DeMaria, Michael Heizer, Mary Miss and Richard Long. Breaking free from the traditions of the studio and the commercial New York gallery scene by venturing out into the wilderness, they introduced the notion that a piece of sculpture could be derived from and be responsive to a specific

82

site. They created monumental, landscape-inspired sculpture that could not be contained in a gallery or sold for profit, and in the process they ushered in a new wave of environmental awareness. Art was reinstated as part of our environment, not an isolated event accessible only to an effete few.

I was especially taken by Robert Smithson's *Spiral Jetty*. I loved the heroic quality of the piece, the romance of the setting and the articulation it gave to a burgeoning environmental awareness. I'm not sure that "site-specific" had been coined as a term yet, but it was evident that the piece resonated with its environment and introduced the idea of time and process into art. It was a living work of art, which, even more heroically, could not be chopped up and sold as an artifact in the New York art market of the late sixties. It was pure. From making discreet landscape objects to shaping the landscape as an integrated artwork and space seemed to me a completely logical sequence.

At the time there were no courses offered in art school on environmental or site-specific art, so after discussions with all kinds of people I decided to try the department of landscape architecture, where I could learn at least about the technical aspects of constructing landscape-art pieces. I began the three-year landscape-architecture program at the University of Michigan and found that in a class of some twenty students, there was only one other student who had an art background. Most, it seemed, had come to school with a religious fervor to save the environment, while I was there to learn how to make big art. Although I too felt that saving the world was a worthy cause, my model for doing so was the Robert Smithson one as opposed to the Ian McHarg model. We may have all shared the same desire to make the world a better place to live, but our ways of achieving it were quite different and mutually misunderstood. When I asked permission to take additional art courses as part of my landscape curriculum, the chairman could not imagine what art had to do with anything, and my request was denied.

My saving grace came when I met Peter Walker in the summer of 1973, when I went out to San Francisco to be a summer-school student at the SWA Group, the office he founded and directed. When the students were invited to his house for dinner, I came across one of Frank Stella's "protractor" paintings. I was completely dumbfounded that a landscape architect would know anything about contemporary

art – and Minimalism to boot. He was the first landscape architect I had met who made any connection to the art world. And, given his stature in the profession, his opinion that art was somehow related to landscape architecture greatly reassured me that perhaps I might find a home within the profession. It was a relief to find a like-minded person in what I considered to be a professional wilderness. His interest in art was a true inspiration to me and kept me going forward in school and ultimately in the profession of landscape architecture.

In school I was also attracted to the works of Minimalist artists, such as Robert Irwin, Robert Morris and Donald Judd, artists who work with the description and manipulation of space through seriality. As landscape encompasses a much greater scale than either painting or sculpture, this effect must be accomplished with economy of means. In their ability to command large spaces with few gestures and materials, the work of the Minimalist artists has much to teach landscape architecture: Richard Long joins a huge valley using only a simple bulldozed line, collapsing the vast space by connecting the viewer with the far side of the mesa; Carl Andre describes a column of space above a perfectly flat plane with plates of industrially discarded metal. In floor pieces by DeMaria and Barry Le Va, the repetition of objects set on a floor mystically elevates the objects while focusing our attention on the visual potential of the flat plane.

In their use of geometry and color, artists such as Leon Polk Smith, Frank Stella, Robert Mangold and Dan Flavin are of particular interest to me. They explore a range of ideas and emotions produced by abstract relationships and delve into the mysticism and symbolism inherent in geometry. The Pop artists – Andy Warhol, Jasper Johns, Roy Lichtenstein and Claes Oldenburg – influence me in their preoccupations with banal, everyday objects and common materials. Insightful, poignant and sympathetic to our common culture, they feed upon its energy and rawness. I respond positively to the hard-edged humor with which they illuminate the stuff of our everyday lives. More recent works, by people like Peter Halley, Richard Artschwager, James Turrell, Dennis Oppenheim, Gary Rieveschl, Philip Taaffe and Damien Hirst, continue to intrigue me.

In addition to the visual inspiration I get from art, I am also attracted to ideas conveyed by art. Ideas must be challenged to prove their viability in a culture. Much art – such as that produced by Kenny Scharf, Jeff Koons and Gordon Matta-Clark, and others such as Vito Acconci and Jenny Holzer – may be important only in that it creates discussion and, in the end, critical self-evaluation. That every work of art or landscape be a timeless masterpiece is ultimately not the question. More importantly, provocative art and design foster an atmosphere of growth through questioning and challenging established standards.

My exposure, education and love of art have taught me that landscape is a fine art and a means of personal expression. It is not enough that the landscape perform as a functional, interstitial fabric flowing under heroic Modernist high-rises, as a mere respite from everyday life, a decoration around some building or a pleasant place to be. Like other art forms, it must provide stimulus for the heart, mind and soul if it is to contribute anything to the culture. It can be an expression of contemporary life and made from a contemporary vocabulary. The landscape can be a medium, as art and architecture, whereby ideas can flower and evolve. In this way, we can develop a meaningful language about our own place, culture and time.

a city at the edge of the forest, a plaza of glacial hills and sawn **logs**

US Courthouse Plaza

Minneapolis, Minnesota 1997
Client: US General Services Administration

"In one sense, this plaza is an ode to the founders of Minnesota," Schwartz says of a city-center space in front of a new federal courthouse designed by Kohn Pedersen Fox. "The first Minnesotans were pioneers and loggers – they used the forest, it's the land of Paul Bunyan. I latched on to the idea that very few people in the state have much contact with logs today."

The silver-stained logs are intended as an evocation of the great timber forests that attracted immigrants and provided the basis for the local economy, which in turn led to the municipal infrastructure which the plaza services. They are also benches: "We needed something for people to sit on – you have to provide plenty of places to sit, or people will not use the space. And since each log starts off fat and gets skinnier, people with long legs can sit comfortably at one end."

The grassed earth mounds (with a core of wire and Styrofoam) are intended to evoke a memory of geological and cultural forms. They suggest a typical Minnesotan field of drumlins, or glacial ridges.

Ranging in height from 3 to 9 feet, the tear-shaped mounds are planted with Jack Pine, a small, stunted, pioneer species common in Minnesota's forest.

The strong diagonal of the logs and the mounds, and the linearity of the striped paving pattern, guide the pedestrian into the courthouse lobby. Minnesota's dramatic seasonal change is reflected in the way the mounds come alive with perennials each spring and summer. Some mounds are blanketed with white narcissus, while others reinforce the paving with stripes of blue scillas. In winter, Minnesota's heavy snows heighten the sculptural effect of the mounds.

The literal deconstruction and symbolic reconstruction of nature is a recurring motif in Schwartz's work, although she says it is not necessarily important that visitors are aware of the specific meanings of such symbolism. That the space is remarkable in itself, and is used and enjoyed by the populace on a sensual, everyday level, is always the paramount consideration.

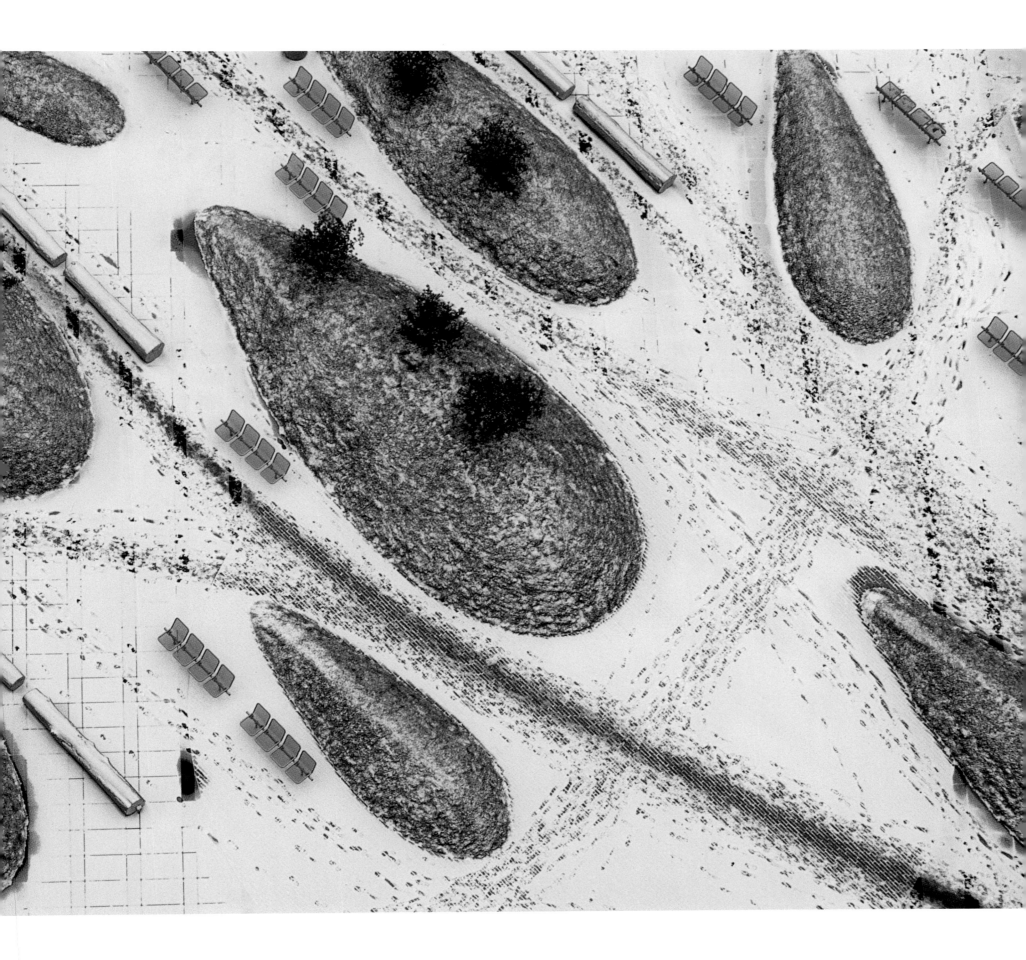

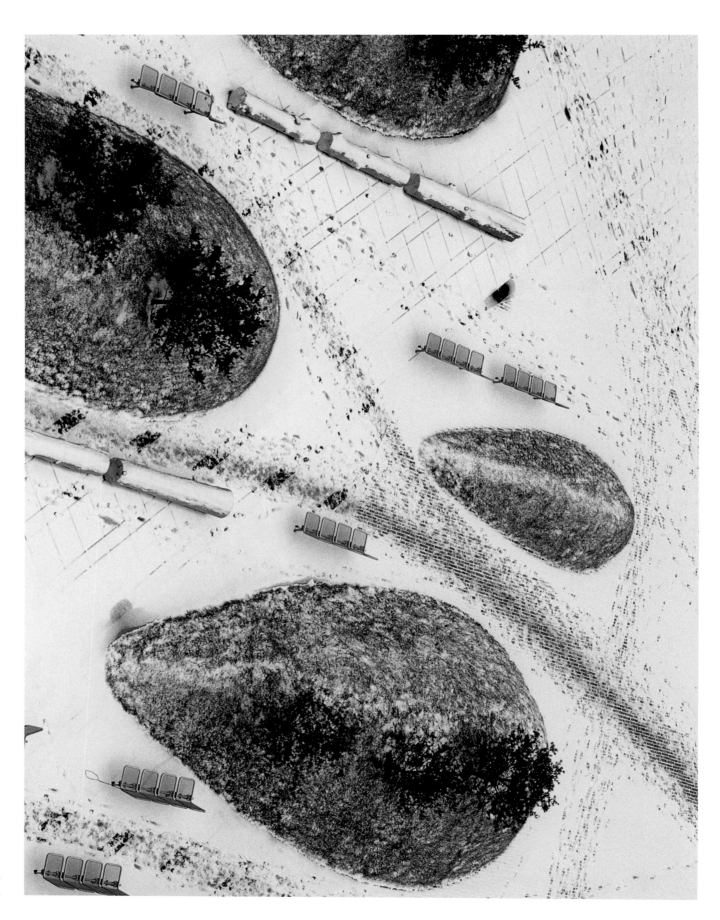

Tracks in the snow create an unplanned
but beautiful image.

The mounds are designed so that their sculptural quality can be read through the heavy blanketing of snow Minneapolis receives every winter.

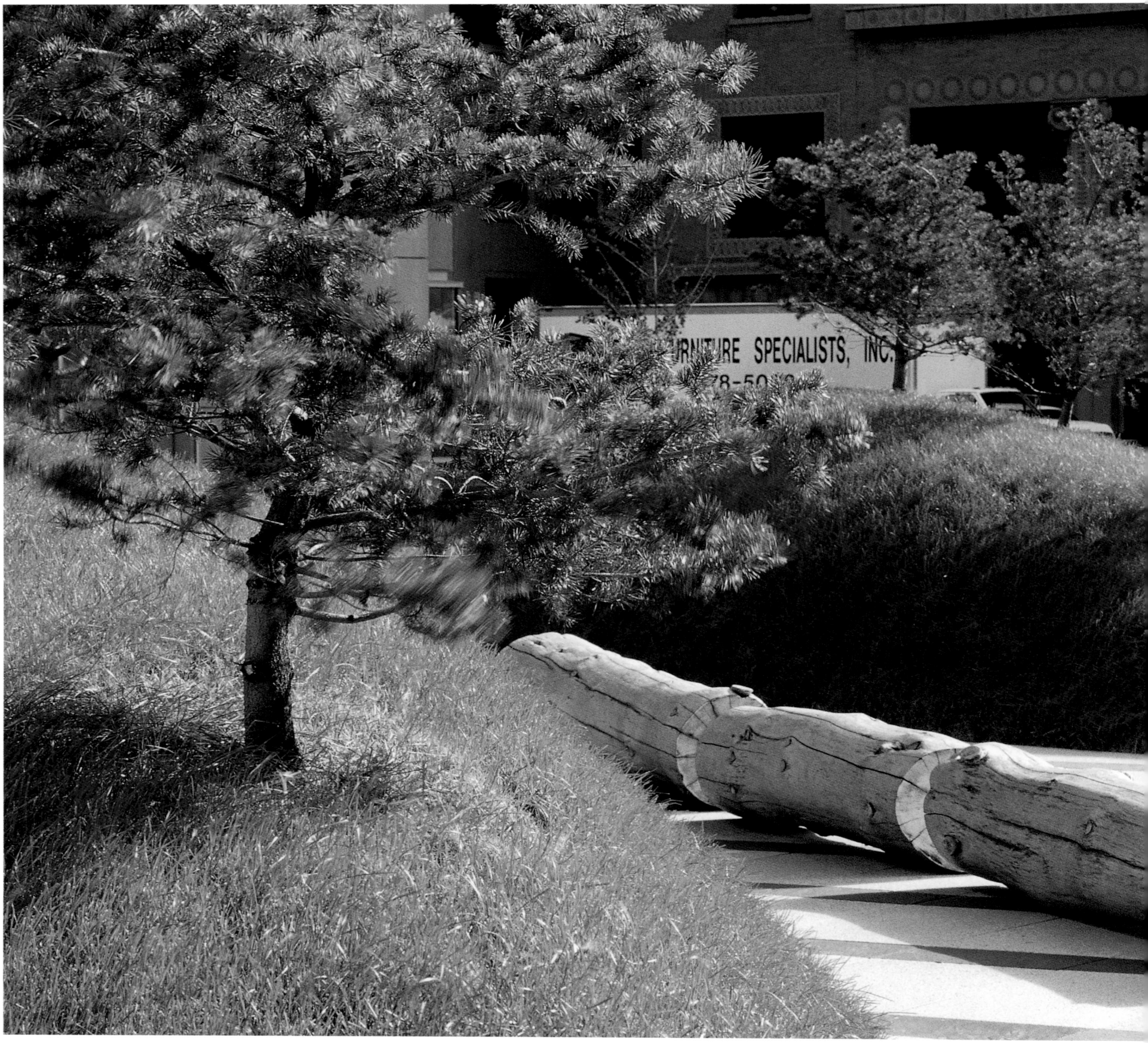
SPECIALISTS, INC.

To deal with the severe weight restrictions, the mounds are highly technical constructions of Styrofoam, mesh and pins. Pockets are left in order to accommodate the root balls of the Jack Pine.

The grass is allowed to grow to 8 in (20 cm) in length, giving the mounds an "animal" shaggy appearance. The Jack Pines are a pioneer species intended as an acknowledgment of the pioneers who settled in Minnesota.

quick, cheap and green = the **garden**

Whitehead Institute Splice Garden

Cambridge, Massachusetts 1986
Client: Whitehead Institute for Biomedical Research

"This is a seminal garden," says Schwartz. "It is a polemic about issues that a lot of our work is based upon."

The 25-by-35-feet (7.6-by-10.7-meters) rooftop garden in Cambridge, Massachusetts, is part of an ambitious art collection assembled for the Whitehead Institute, a microbiology research center. The site was a lifeless space atop a nine-story office building designed by Boston architects Goody, Clancy & Associates. Its tiled roof surface and high surrounding walls conspired to create a dark, inhospitable space, overlooked by a classroom and a faculty lounge. The lounge offered access to the courtyard, making it a potential lunch venue.

"For this commission, everyone wanted it green," Schwartz says, "and they wanted it quickly. But the structure wasn't strong enough for soil, so there was no opportunity for plants. When the building was being designed, no one demanded that space be maintained to encourage life. I was shocked that there was nothing up there that could sustain life. There was not even a water supply. No money was allocated to maintain a garden or its structure. So this piece is all about the idea of the garden, and about what one expects from a garden – this mantra that it should be quick, cheap and green. We all want to see green but we don't want to spend money on it – yet we really love nature, right? This garden was an angry response to that.

It was: 'If you want green and you don't want to pay for it, here it is.'"

All the plants in the garden are plastic. The clipped hedges, which double as seating, are rolled steel covered in Astroturf. The green colors are composed of raked expanses of colored aquarium gravel and paint. Schwartz explains: "If a garden is a representation of nature, then this is a re-representation of nature. Something that won't weigh anything, makes no demands and will not involve having to keep things alive. It's like human beings who won't make a commitment."

The garden also became a cautionary tale related to the work carried out by the Institute, and specifically about a danger inherent in gene splicing: the possibility of creating a monster. So in a sense the garden is a monster – it is a joining together, like Siamese twins, of gardens from different cultures. One side is based on a French Renaissance garden, the other on a traditional Japanese garden. The elements that compose these gardens have been distorted: the rocks typically found in a Zen garden are composed of topiary pom-poms from the French garden. Other plants, such as palms and conifers, are in strange and unfamiliar associations. Some plants project off the vertical surface of the wall; others teeter precariously on the wall's top edge.

The French part of the garden is based upon the famous hedge gardens of Villandry [below].

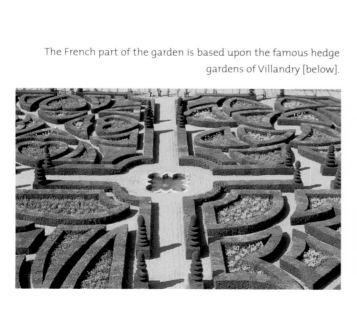

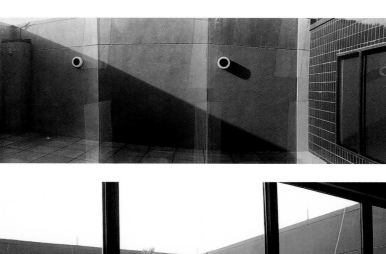

The view to the garden from the classroom [above] provides a visual puzzle for the students.

The line down the middle is a key element of the design. It is the "splice line" along which the two disparate gardens are joined.

The image below is taken from the famous garden of Ryoan-ji, the Japanese garden upon which the "Zen" half of the Splice Garden is based. However, instead of sculptural rocks, French topiary balls are used, further confusing an interpretation.

making a farm into a **sculpture**

Winslow Farms Conservancy

Hammonton, New Jersey 1996
Client: Henry McNeil

This large-scale agricultural project was seen by Schwartz as a marriage between art and the necessary practicalities of reclamation and ecology. The 600-acre (243-hectare) McNeil property is an estate located within the New Jersey pine barrens; it contains a diverse range of landscape conditions including dense forests, gradually rolling topography, and a 75-acre (30-hectare) abandoned clay quarry that holds mineral-rich turquoise water and is surrounded by virtually sterile soils. Henry McNeil is creating an artist's retreat at the estate, while maintaining it as a working farm and as a place to train champion labrador field dogs. Martha Schwartz, Inc. was called in to contribute to a project aimed at transforming the site into an area of exceptional beauty through artistic intervention and enhancement of the landscape.

Through an intimate collaborative process with the client and contractors, working directly on site, the project was initially approached as a subtractive process. Spaces were carved into the site by calculated, selective clearing. The site was graded to enhance the rolling landscape and create juxtapositions with sculpted forms. Soils were amended to support plants and crops, which were composed formally to create a work conceived as an intriguing dialogue with the "wild" nature of the landscape. Paths and roads have been carefully re-sited to influence perceptions of the landscape.

"We tried to sculpt the space out of the existing pines and the farm fields where organic exotic crops are grown," Schwartz says. "The soil in the quarry is very poor and leached of nutrients, so when we chopped down trees, we made them into a kind of mulch to reconstitute the soil. We regenerated that landscape on several levels."

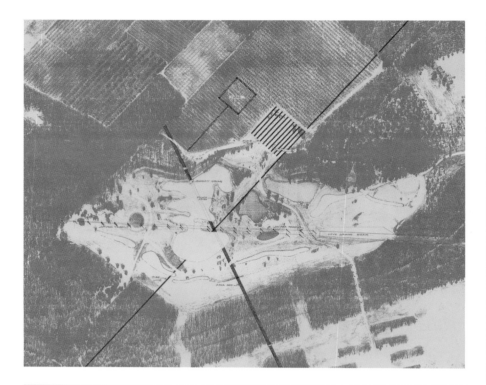

A series of axis lines were created through the pines. These organized a series of outdoor rooms and allowed long vistas through the forest.

This is a reclaimed clay quarry [left] that had been further degraded by dirt biking. The quarry was cleared out and repaired. The clay soil was reconstituted using the wood chips created by chopping the wood that was cleared. It is now a refuge for birds and other wildlife that had abandoned the area. The project was a substantial process by which spaces and structure were created through clearing the trees [below].

ghosts of the everglade **light** the way

Broward County Civic Arena
Fort Lauderdale, Florida   1998

The plaza in front of the home stadium of the Florida Panthers ice hockey team was conceived as a way of integrating the building with the vast, empty, open space in front of it. "Because of the very tight budget, we could not put any structures on the plaza," Schwartz explains. "So we went for something with scale, that could be seen from a distance and impact the plaza as much as possible."

Sixteen sculptural canopies of steel and colored vinyl fabric recall the displaced Everglade trees that once occupied the site of the arena – in the original planned project, living royal palms were to be used. Instead, the two rows of virtual trees indicate the stadium entrance; the canopies glow at night and light the way for visitors. A striped paving pattern, generated from the building's geometry, reinforces the pattern of the canopies. The much-reduced scheme was nicknamed (by Martha Schwartz, Inc.) "the flying saucer plaza."

"We had many suggestions for bringing the landscape down to the scale of people, but we were not able to do that," says Schwartz. "In the end, we could just do enough to engineer some kind of relationship between the building and plaza." But Schwartz says that the revised scheme has integrity and its own logic, and visitors should not be able to guess the painful genesis of the piece: "For a dancer," she says, "when you're out there on stage, you're supposed to look weightless. You don't want to know what the ballerina has gone through to be able to do that."

Various alternatives were proposed for the plaza [above].

The light structures and plastic discs are part of a series of elements for the plaza, many of which were never completed. The discs, or "flying saucers," have become icons for Fort Lauderdale and their images used on promotional posters for the city.

mounds by the roadside entice travelers

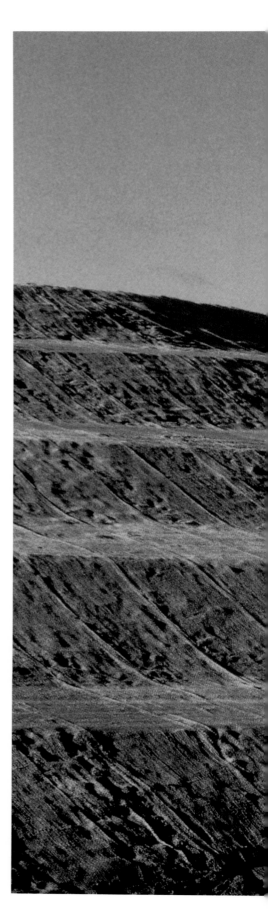

Geraldton Mine Project

Geraldton, Ontario, Canada   1998
Client: Barrick Gold

Geraldton is a small town of some 700 inhabitants, about 200 miles (322 kilometers) north-east of Thunder Bay in Ontario. The MacLeod Goldmine operated from 1943 to 1972, and was the last working mine in the region. Its legacy was some 14 million tons of tailings or industrial slag, which form shallow hills up to 30 feet (9 meters) high over an area of 170 acres (69 hectares).

Martha Schwartz, Inc. was engaged to landscape the tailings, with a minimum of earthmoving, as part of the town's effort to spur economic development. "It turned out that Geraldton was 3 kilometers off the Trans-Canadian Highway – the last east-west road in North America," Schwartz says. "They realized the town could derive an economy based on passing tourism. The problem was the visual quality of the land after the activities of earlier mining companies (but not Barrick Gold, the company that commissioned the project).

It was so degraded and ugly – and you can see it all from the highway.

"We attended to all the issues around clearing it up, plus the question of: 'How do we make it interesting, so that people driving by want to stop?' We needed an intersection that was compelling enough for people to want to turn off the highway, go to the town, eat in a restaurant and maybe spend the night. In North America, only engineers do reclamation projects; we wanted to add a visual element. This piece is like a giant billboard in that sense."

The firm sculpted the tailings nearest the road into compelling landforms that now constitute an intriguing gateway to the town, celebrating rather than negating its industrial history. Six to twelve inches (15 to 30 centimeters) of peat topsoil were added to disturbed areas to aid revegetation, and the planting plan focuses primarily on native grasses, especially those golden in color. The landform was designed to be more than just a powerful visual feature. Trails invite one to walk, birdwatch, mountain bike, snowboard, or sled. Of special importance to the area's tourism is the inclusion of snowmobile trails, and there are plans to expand the adjacent golf course from nine holes to eighteen, onto the tailings. Schwartz: "We wanted to do something that did not fit in. High contrast. The intention was not to blend into nature."

The earthforms have just been completed and are without their plantings of different colored grasses. This "moonscape" is meant to contrast with the existing flat landscape so as to encourage people to stop and explore, and perhaps to bring them into the small town of Geraldton to shop or eat.

Two schemes were presented to the townspeople: one very rectilinear, the other curvaceous and flowing. The curvy one was selected and built.

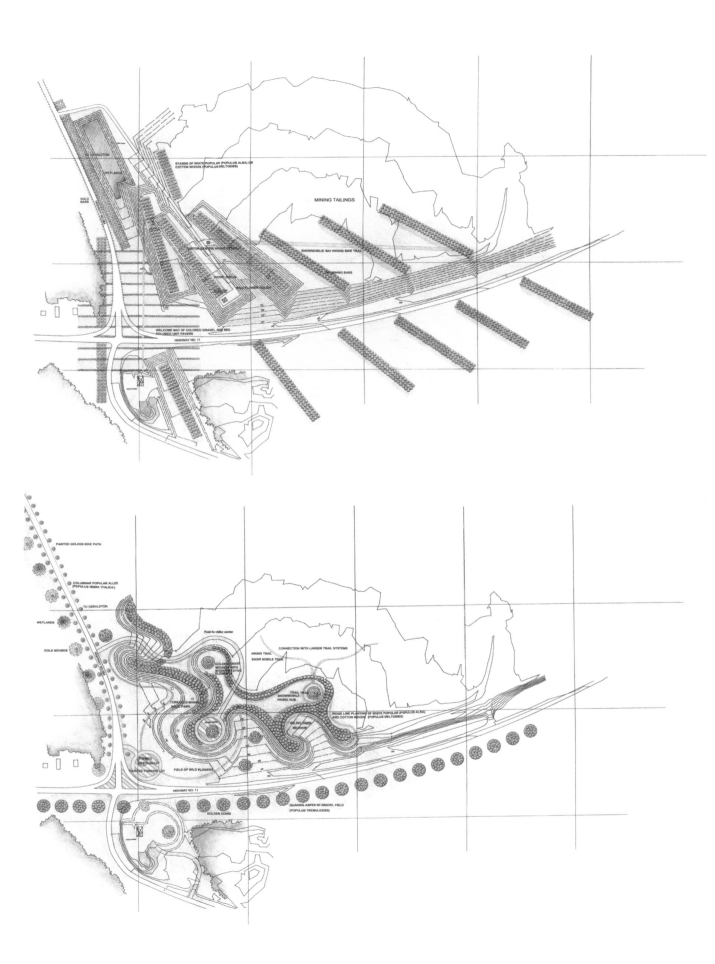

The drawings produced by the computer for
quantity calculations are works of graphic merit
in their own right.

an abstract **willow**, facsimile of nature

Bo 01 City of Tomorrow Exhibition

Malmö, Sweden   2001
European Housing Expo

"I like shows and exhibitions," says Schwartz. "It's my background as a printmaker and artist. Given the medium, a painter can move through ideas much more quickly. The materiality affects the rate at which ideas can be formulated, so the art world produces visual ideas much faster than architecture."

The willow tree of the future which constituted this installation is situated amid a real willow grove. The steel central pole or "tree trunk" supports a stainless-steel wire canopy which holds strands of branches of green mylar (an extraordinarily strong polyester film), which get shorter towards the center of the tree. This "stepping up" of the mylar strands creates a hallowing, room-like space, one of the most extraordinary qualities of a weeping willow. The fake willow also recreates the sounds the wind makes through the leaves of a real tree, and the mystery is heightened by sounds of a crying woman coming from within the canopy. The ground at the base of the tree is

seasonless, durable, green Astroturf. This abstract willow does not depend upon water, soil, temperature, or sunlight. It grows anywhere in the world, in any season. Its prefabrication is intended to echo the way facsimiles and the virtual are seen to be replacing what is considered real or authentic.

The temporary nature of such exhibition and expo installations is not seen as a drawback by Schwartz, rather as a way of "prodding the development of landscape." She asks: "When you see a performance at the ballet, does it have no effect on the culture when it is finished? Is there no inherent artistic virtue in something that does not last long? You don't create a sense of place through time alone. It's all about the idea, how something is expressed. If something is truly beautiful and moves us, it can change us. If it can do both – move you emotionally and last a long time physically – it is a treasure. That tree was a beautiful thing and it will last in people's minds."

116

The "gardens" in the fair had to be 10 x 10 meters (33 x 33 feet). The abstract willow was a 10-meter cube of green nylon curtains which represented a mechanical "willow of the future" set within a grove of "Swedish bamboo," a willow used to rejuvenate the soil.

The strands of nylon made a luscious sound – like a willow tree. Inside the steel column was the sound of a woman softly weeping.

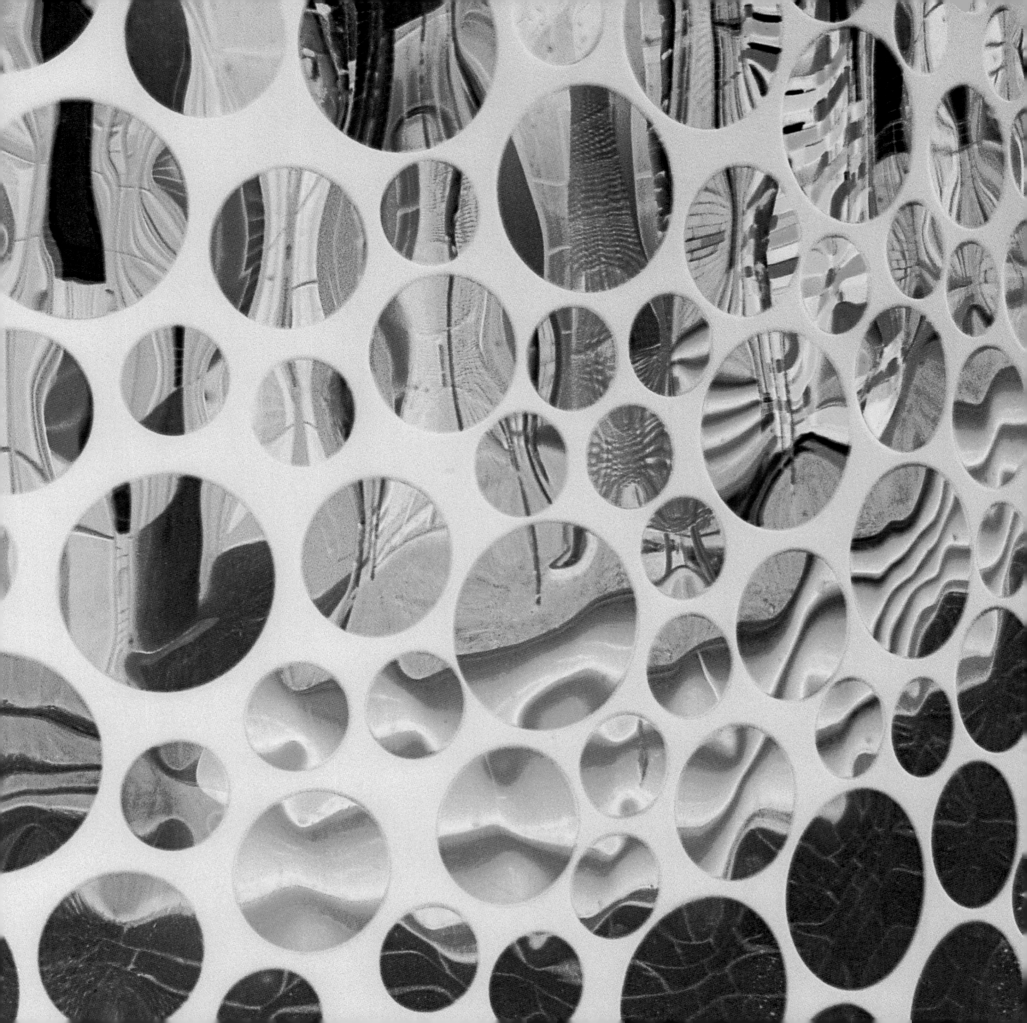

[My Mission by Martha Schwartz]

Although dramatic improvements have been made in landscape architecture during the twenty years I have been practicing, the profession's relationship to art remains tenuous and ill-defined, for both practitioners and the general public. Perhaps because the profession of landscape architecture is loosely defined, its relationship to art will always be ambiguous. Some practitioners view it as antithetical to art because they believe that humankind shouldn't violate "nature," and that the job of the landscape architect is to protect and save the earth from human intervention. The general public generally sees "nature" as somehow everything not human, where a well-designed landscape is one in which you don't detect "the hand of man." This causes great tension within the profession, given that we are building our environment and we all live within these built environments. The hand of man is everywhere, whether we like it or not.

In spite of the demand for landscape architects to create pretty pastoral scenes, we are dealing with ever-increasing human interventions in the environment. Our environment, now, is what and where we decide it to be. We build the landscape we live in and can therefore either design it or abdicate the design process and let nature take its course. For architects, the design of our environment is the single most important task we have for the twenty-first century.

The landscape architect's job is to design the landscape. We are to imbue it with form, meaning and beauty. We are to create context, memory and place. We are in charge of shaping the very human artifact of landscape. We must therefore look to the traditions that will give us history and context for the expression of visual ideas, we must look to art. The artists are the true researchers of the visual realm.

Viewing the landscape as a cultural art form, like architecture, painting and sculpture, demands that training in art and art history be a fundamental part of the education of landscape architects. I have tried to incorporate my education and background in art into my projects throughout my career. My work has always dealt with a variety of outdoor spaces and with complicated programmatic issues. Every work is "site-specific": the solution is unique to that site and can be derived only from that site. I do not make objects, but produce an environment where the art and landscape components are indistinguishable. I see the landscape as a vehicle for self-expression.

My work is an attempt to address the many needs inherent in designing landscapes – programmatic, formal, aesthetic, stylistic – while trying to satisfy the ever-present urge to create something that is my own. Like most artists and architects, I wish to leave a mark, something that, at best, bespeaks whatever uniqueness I can bring to a place or that at least shows that "I was here." I see landscape as a medium and a vehicle for personal expression, much as a painter would view a box of paints.

The landscapes we live and work in are determined by us, so the design of the landscape determines the quality of our physical environment. To serve the role our manifold landscapes play in our lives – backyards, highway corridors, shopping-mall parking lots, city and suburban streets, service corridors, railroad corridors, strips, plazas, courtyards, waterfronts – they must be designed to accommodate all the uses people bring to them, *as well as* to respect or enhance ecological standards and practices. Because our landscapes are cultural artifacts, their design can be as rich and diverse as the people who design and inhabit them. These often overlooked or underfunded spaces can be designed to convey a narrative, express a point of view, conjure a feeling and mood, be a neutral backdrop for more vivid human activities, and even mimic natural landscapes, if this is a desired effect.

Ever since the Bagel Garden, my work has often been controversial or characterized as "unecological" or "anti-nature." Because of the use of artificial or manmade materials, such as plastics or glass, intense

My Mission by Martha Schwartz

124

colors and strong geometries, critics wrongly attribute to my designs a lack of ecological responsibility. I am often stunned by these criticisms, particularly because they come most often from within the profession, where styles such as naturalism or "eco-rev" (eco-revelatory) are fashionable, easily understood and highly marketable. It is falsely believed that if a landscape looks "natural," it is in fact natural, ecological or even sustainable. But designing ecologically does not determine form or style – the two *can* each be completely independent of the other. It is important

that we build our environment in an ecologically sensitive manner, but the formal expression of the landscape, like other cultural art forms, is open to individual interpretation, just as architecture and art.

The designs my office has created always place people at center stage and give foremost consideration to how people use the landscape. We begin by researching the site and analyzing the natural systems that might have an impact on the site, such as geological substructure. A site also has a cultural history, while local customs, politics and sociology play a role too. The research presents a multilayered picture of the site that then begins to suggest an approach. The most important objective is to create a space about which people care, enjoy using and are motivated to sustain. "Sustainable" design is useless if the people using the space do not care enough about it to maintain it. If you design spaces that have no character to which people can relate, they will not survive over time: visual character is a large factor in "sustainability." Designing ecologically does not dictate any particular style.

I have always been interested in exploring new or unconventional materials. Like the Pop artists, I embrace the materials used and found in everyday life. It is important to me to do so, for these are the materials out of which our quotidian world is being constructed and lived. Our democratic and middle-class culture is one of junk materials, and if we are to participate in this culture, we must learn to elevate and love them. After all, if Robert Rauschenberg can take refuse out of a garbage can and through his imagination and art transform this garbage into something of beauty, we can, as landscape architects, transform our banal environments into spaces of beauty and character.

We are often called upon to design spaces that will represent communities or will create a "there, there," a destination, a place that captures a collective image. Creating places that are memorable, describable and project a strong image can serve a community, an interest group, a city, even a country. Such spaces often occupy central or high-profile areas so the design has to present a symbol to the outside world. The landscape reflects upon the people of the community and in the end forms a self-image to the individuals of that community. For me it is an extreme privilege to create such a place, so our landscapes must function at the highest level, be of particular use (such as the provision of seating, viewing, congregating, biking, hiking, skating), be accessible, be ecologically and sustainably designed to survive the multi-level bureaucratic

approval processes, and withstand the inevitable "value engineering."
A landscape's most important function, however, is to serve the
human psyche.

  Unfortunately, people have a very limited notion of what a
landscape is. Most people conjure up a forest, waterfalls, the prairie,
and other pristine or primeval untouched natural environments. In
the city, landscape is thought of as parks, waterfronts and plazas.
Although these spaces are landscapes, landscape need not be
confined to parks, waterfronts and gardens: it must include all the
spaces found outside the building footprint – alleys, highways,
sidewalks, parking lots, strip malls, suburban tracts, utility corridors –
all are constructed artifacts. Our landscape, contrary to our fantasy of
the wilderness, is what we determine it to be.

community space to honor privacy and individuality

Gifu Kitagata Apartments

Kitagata, Japan   2000
Client: Gifu Prefectural Government

A courtyard project, part of an experiment in "feminism in housing design" that also includes four apartment buildings designed by Akiko Takahashi, Kazuyo Sejima, Christine Hawley, and Elizabeth Diller. "This project is only 'feminist' because women did it," Schwartz asserts. "We didn't do a feminist treatise, nor do I believe that the product was something only women would have created. The mayor of Gifu wanted something attractive to prove the point that low-cost housing need not be punitive. Arata Isozaki, the architect of the scheme, was asked to choose and preside over the team of designers. I was told that he wanted the project done by women because he believed that given the very small amount of space for the apartments (700 square feet, 65 square meters), women might do a better job thinking about the interior spaces. For the landscape, I thought a lot about different kinds of families – those with old people, those with children, and we created a variety of small but age-specific mini-landscapes where everyone could be in his or her own space while all being together. That is the idea behind it."

Rice paddies existed on this site, before its present use for housing. The sculptural structure of raised dikes and sunken paddies provides the metaphor for creating a raised platform on which a series of sunken garden rooms are set. These rooms offer a variety of opportunities for passive enjoyment or active play including water features, children's play opportunities, and public art. In the Willow Court, a sunken, flooded area with willow trees and wetland vegetation is made accessible by a wooden boardwalk. This is an area that provides privacy from the surrounding apartments when the trees mature and is intended as a meeting place for lovers. The Four Seasons Garden, a place for teenagers, is a series of four miniature

gardens that capture the spirit of each of the seasons and are enclosed by colored Plexiglas walls. ("We looked at them as lanterns," Schwartz explains.) In the Stone Garden, a circular fountain with stepping stones and concrete rocks that spit water at irregular intervals creates a children's play pool. The other garden rooms are the Cherry Forecourt, Iris Canal, Dance Floor, Children's Playground, Sports Court, Water Rill, and Bamboo Garden. Each of these rooms provides a different experiential opportunity.

"We wanted to make areas that catered for different age groups," Schwartz says. "Little children love some of the spaces, while the older kids, the 12 to 14 year olds, love that pink fountain. Then there is the more contemplative willow grove, which is too boring for little kids. But it's hidden, which teenagers like. The wooden dance-floor was requested by the older people."

The fountain of pink concrete lumps came about by accident. "Originally the idea was for a big bowl-shaped fountain of raw pink-granite rocks," Schwartz explains. "That was too expensive, so we moved to concrete and thought about a more sculptural rendition. We commissioned these concrete forms from a Japanese firm, and the next thing we knew we got these photographs and the concrete rocks were painted pink. I think they took our terminology of 'pink-granite' too literally. We were shocked at the images of these pink...things. The men in our office were most shocked. It was a really embarrassing moment. So I took a vote on whether to keep them. All the men said repaint them, to a man. All the women said they looked nice pink. There were more women than men, so I kept them pink. It was a cross-cultural misunderstanding that worked out brilliantly."

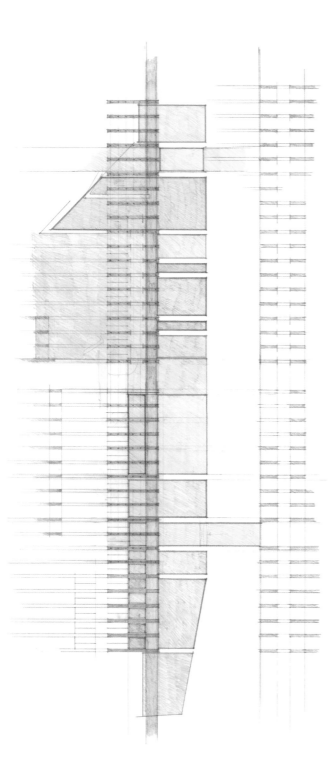

The communal space was long and linear. It had to serve many types
of household – single, married, elderly, working and unemployed. The
multiple small gardens responded to the many types of space
required by the inhabitants.

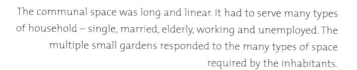

This end shows the community center which is largely used by the elderly and mothers with small children.

Four boxes have been designed as small gardens, each representing one of the four seasons: yellow for spring, green for summer, red for fall and blue for winter.

The boat fountain is made from the local
ceramics for which Gifu is well known. It is
a shallow fountain for small children with
a sculpture by Aiko Miyakawa.

The plate of "pink things" came about as a happy misunderstanding. Originally these were specified as stones of pink granite, but they arrived as concrete forms.

a process of addition: does **more** mean less?

Stella Garden

Bala-Cynwyd, Pennsylvania 1980

Martha Schwartz describes this as a very early experimental garden, one of the first of her career. "Peter Walker [Schwartz's then business partner and husband] encouraged me to try things, so I experimented and did installations. I was told I was unprofessional not waiting for someone to pay me to do these things, but I didn't care. If you're an artist, you just do it."

The space was her mother's dark 20-feet (6-meters) square backyard, where Schwartz experimented with a new approach to design. "I had been looking at the work of Frank Stella – he had gone from minimalist work to a series called *The Birds*, which were these glittery, colorful collages. So I thought I would do the opposite of minimalism, too, and just keep adding and adding. So I collected things, junk – chicken wire, Plexiglas, logs, colored concrete blocks, ladders – and drove it down from Boston."

Since conventional gardening was not an option – "My mother doesn't like to go into the garden; it was really a garden to look at" – colored Plexiglas scraps were used to fabricate the garden walls and provide color. A 10-by-10-feet platform sits askew, but on an axis to the two poles, that support a chicken-wire cloud which is the entrance gate to the garden. The patio surface is colored with gravels, mimicking the colors of the fence, and interacting with the colored shadows that the Plexiglas casts. A table of wire-glass rests on four cinder-blocks. The concrete stoop, which leads to the back door, has been extended further into the garden. Turquoise and green striped Astroturf leads up the stairs, up the wall flanking the back door and continues under the eaves of the terracotta roof which marks the back entrance. The concrete stairwell leading down to the basement, and the exposed stone foundations of the house, are painted a light lavender, and the five trash cans that sit at the entrance to the garden have been painted with glitter, so they sparkle in the sunshine.

The experiment taught Schwartz that this was not the way she wanted to work: "As much fun as I had with this additive policy, it was not something I was comfortable with. It was not as satisfying as having an idea and using the subtractive method to get to the important things."

Stella Schwartz (the designer's mother) as client.

138

The objective was to make a garden by adding more and more to the composition. A lot of material was retrieved from the client's garage, painted and placed in the garden. The windows are painted as different sized rectangles. The "garden" color comes from Plexiglas panels.

At night the Plexiglas panels glowed.

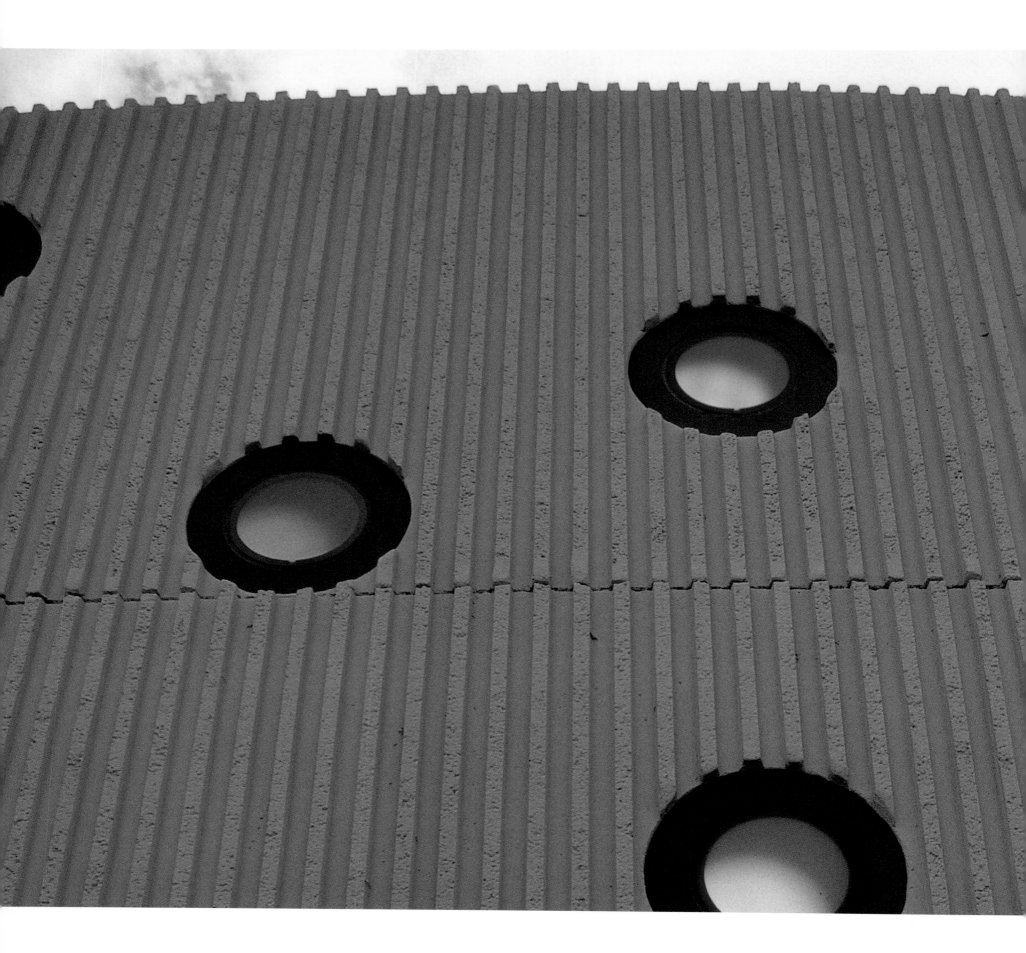

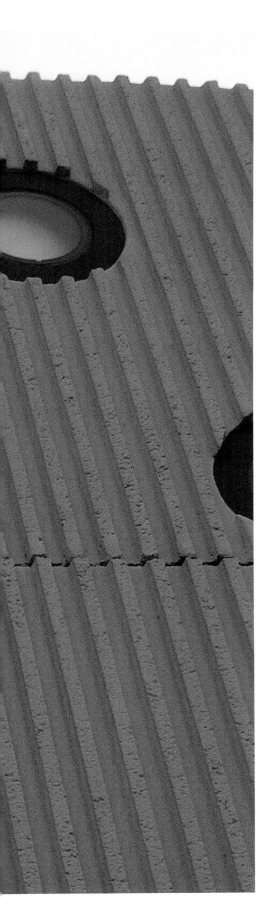

colored portholes add **light** to a wavy wall

Miami International Airport Sound Attenuation Wall

Miami, Florida 1996
Client: Metro-Dade Art in Public Places Award

A mile-long wall by a public roadway at the northern boundary of Miami's international airport was built as much for security as for noise reduction, and local residents were incensed by its presence. Martha Schwartz, Inc. were called in to transform it into something people could enjoy.

"The solution was light," says Schwartz. "The wall faces north, so the outer face was always going to be in shade. So I decided to puncture holes in it to let the light from the south shine through. We devised six different concrete panels with randomly spaced colored portholes.

We put some panels in upside-down to further randomize the pattern." By reshaping the top of the wall and regrading the landscape at its base, the sound wall undulates at a height of 25–30 feet (7.6–9 meters) down the mile-long stretch of roadway. At the entrance to the airport, the holes organize into a grid. This change in pattern makes the holes appear to pulsate and implies motion.

"The wall was so successful that the local newspaper made it its logo," Schwartz says. "There were fears that people would try to shoot out the glass, but that hasn't happened."

The sound wall runs along the northern boundary of the Miami Dade International Airport. The art component was an "add-on" to the wall after it became controversial among residents of the bordering neighborhood.

power: electrical and political

Power Lines

Gelsenkirchen, Germany 1999
International Building Exhibition Emscher Park; artists: Martha Schwartz and Markus Jatsch

An artwork commissioned as part of a ten-year International Building Exhibition funded by the German government, intended to regenerate the Ruhr Valley culturally and economically. The site, Mechtenberg, is the only natural hill in the coal-mining area of the Emscher region – there are other "hills," but they are in fact slagheaps from coalmining.

"It's spooky up there," says Schwartz of the ragged black locust forest on top of the hill. "The top of the hill is said to have been an ancient site for Odin worshippers. In the middle of the forest there is a blackened hulk of a statue to Bismarck. The area is still criss-crossed by electrical power lines and was one of the most heavily industrialized and environmentally degraded areas in the world. That's where the 'power' issue came from: the power of electricity and the political power resulting from Bismarck's unification of Germany."

A geometric series of narrow cornfields, shaped as "dashes," was planted under the electric power lines connecting the towering pylons. Emphasizing the topography, the dashes of corn ran parallel to the power lines, like energy radiating off them and structuring the farmer's field. The Red Corridor, defined by two walls made from stacked haybales wrapped in colored sheeting, marks the axis from the Bismarck monument. This hallway connects the Bismarck statue to the point of intersection with the electricity power lines. The hallway is colored red, a "power" color and the color of blood. The space of the hallway is very narrow, forcing visitors to think consciously about who can pass when two people meet head on. The Black Room is located at the intersection of the Bismarck and power line axes. It is a circular room contained by stacked haybales wrapped in black plastic. The floor is made of coal. Schwartz called this room the black heart of the installation.

The installation lasted one month, the corn was harvested to help pay for it, and a party was held in the Black Room: bratwurst was barbecued and Marilyn Manson music was played.

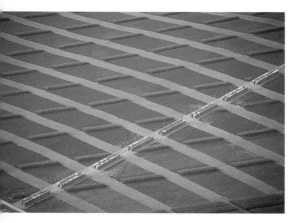

The temporary art installation was on a functioning piece of farmland in the Ruhr Valley of Germany. The materials were corn, clover and baled hay.

The axis to the Bismarck statue and the axis of the electrical power lines, delineated by a thick line of corn, intersected at the black circular room Schwartz describes as "the heart of darkness."

146

The Bismarck axis is a one-person-wide corridor made from bales of
hay wrapped in red plastic made especially for this piece. Schwartz
describes this as the "blood" axis, where power is established in the
small social interactions required when determining who should walk
first through the corridor, and who needs to move out of the way.

dreams of **escape** reflected in a fragmented reality

King County Jailhouse Garden
Seattle, Washington 1987
Client: King County Arts Commission

An art project commissioned by King County under its 1 per cent for art ordinance, the garden plaza contained no plants because there was no money for maintenance. "Having a landscape is like having a pet," says Schwartz. "You have to feed it. If you can't, get a stuffed animal." The garden plaza had to function as an entrance lobby for the jailhouse (which lacked one): a place where visitors, lawyers and workers could meet and wait. The prisoners have no access to this area, although they can look down on it.

The plaza is a colorful and superficially light-hearted formal garden complete with hedges, topiary, parterres and fountain – all constructed out of precast concrete and ceramic tile. A large ceramic mural on the jailhouse wall represents a gate.

"The garden is a metaphor for escape," Schwartz explains.

"It's a drawing, basically, of a classical garden parterre, with an axis and a cross-axis. I used that to create a center for the site – there was no heart to the space. It had to function as a foyer, and a place for children to play on brightly colored objects. But I wanted it to be a surreal space, on the edge of a bad dream, to feel like it was almost falling apart." Schwartz's practice considers escapism to be an undesirable design prerogative, and intimations of perfection were felt to be inappropriate in such a setting. The tile fragments suggest that the garden is in a process of disintegration – a recognition of the chaos, danger and fragility of the prisoners' lives. Schwartz acknowledges that it is an emotionally charged work: "The really good stuff, the memorable stuff, is driven by emotion."

The classical arrangement of a parterre garden, which has a strong
center, is imagined in a space that has no real certainty. The design,
as Schwartz describes it, is a surreal review of a garden that is
starting to disintegrate and has the aura of a bad dream.

The Euclidean "topiary" forms seem to be floating independently of the structured garden surface. Unlike the brightly colored pastels of the rest of the garden, these forms are a dark olive, imparting an ominous presence to the plaza.

the mundane and the beautiful clash with the tragedy of **slavery**

Spoleto Festival

Charleston, South Carolina   1997
Client: Spoleto Festival USA

A temporary art installation, entitled "Field Work," was shown at the McLeod Plantation, a 19th-century cotton estate where six slave cabins still stand in meadows that were once cotton fields. At right angles to the allée of oaks lining the main drive to the house, rows of metal poles supporting 6-by-9-feet (1.8-by-2.7 meters) panels of white cotton scrim created narrow "yards" around each slave cabin. Field paint was used to white out large panels of grass between the rows of poles and fluttering cotton.

Its superficial resemblance to a clothes-line attracted many visitors to the piece, but the context of place and the history of slavery lent it transcendent meaning. The whited-out grass sections leading to the slave cabins became poignant, and in the ghostly, billowing sheets, some visitors also found echoes of the sailing ships that brought slaves from Africa. "I wanted to do something that commented upon the serious issues, but at the same time had a beauty that transcended that," Schwartz says. "You think about what slavery was like, and then there's the beauty of the site itself, the romantic quality. Both of these things exist. It's emotionally difficult."

Schwartz sees no fundamental difference between artwork such as this and her landscape projects. "We don't approach it differently – it's just a longer time continuum with landscape," she explains. "With landscape, there are so many practical considerations that have to be met, and you're going to get a different product when you start ticking off the practicalities. With a commissioned artwork you are freer artistically – but free is the word, because no money is involved."

The hung cotton "sheets" helped to illustrate the changing moods of the day. They hung heavy with moisture in the mornings and evenings, and flapped vertically with the afternoon breeze.

White is the color of death for many Africans. The sheets also provided a foil for the magnificent shadow patterns cast by the aged oak trees leading up to the "Big House" of the plantation.

golden **frogs** at prayer in the mall

Rio Shopping Center

Atlanta, Georgia   1988
Client: Ackerman and Company

158

The twin aims of this project are curiosity and laughter. An army of 350 gilded frogs ranged in orderly lines faces a 40-feet (12-meters) geodesic dome, as the focus of an Atlanta shopping center designed by Miami-based Arquitectonica. "Humor is important in life," says Schwartz. "In the Jewish culture, it's really important: I was raised in a pretty funny family." Schwartz points out that humor can be an effective means of delivering a serious point of view or venting anger, although in this case the frogs do neither.

"This is a shopping environment," she continues. "It's supposed to be fun and alternative. The shopping center is sited next to a highway and lots of cheap buildings and hoardings. It was a lonely spot and needed illuminating. This was our billboard."

The first level of shops opens onto a courtyard 10 feet below the street. Overlapping squares of lawn, paving, stones, and architecture form the basis of the design. The squares are layered with other geometric pieces – lines, circles, spheres, cubes. These elements meet in a black pool which is striated by lines of fiber-optics that glow at night. A floating path, reflected above by an architectural bridge, connects one side of the shopping area to the other. The frogs are set in a grid at the base of the globe that is stationed on a slope connecting the road to the courtyard. Alternating stripes of riprap (loose broken stones) and grass cover the slope. The grid of frogs continues down the slope and through the pool, all facing the giant sphere, as if they are paying homage. The globe, which has been planted with vines, houses a mist fountain. A square plaza beyond this focal point forms a meeting place that includes a circular bar, a bamboo grove that punctures the roof, and a video installation by artist Dara Birnbaum.

But why frogs? "I don't like to tell the secret of the frogs," Schwartz jokes. "The fact is, we were left without any kind of money for this phase of the design. There were supposed to be water features in this shallow rectangular pool which was inherently boring. The frog idea was an act of desperation. We rang round Atlanta trying to find some kind of garden sculpture that we could repeat. Some guy had 350 concrete frogs, so we used them. It could have been something else."

The Rio plaza was an outdoor space
attendant to a newly designed strip mall.
The landscape was an ode to shopping.

Three hundred and fifty gold-painted frogs studded the shallow pond and the rolling landscape that linked the street to the shopping mall one level down. The frogs were a quick fix for a landscape that had "lost" its construction budget and could not afford the fountains designed for the space.

a **sequence** of spaces that explodes into a landscape

Dickenson Residence

Santa Fe, New Mexico   1991
Client: Nancy Dickenson

Nancy Dickenson is a folk-art collector whose solitary hilltop retreat commands wide views of the New Mexico Badlands and the Sangre de Cristo mountains. The existing layout of house and garden required visitors to pass through a series of unconnected spaces to reach the rear terrace and its uninterrupted views.

"I felt an order needed to be imposed on the loosey-goosey Santa Fe adobe style," Schwartz explains. The space was replanned as a logical sequence of indoor and outdoor rooms, beginning with a car parking area, moving down into a formal entrance courtyard, through the living area and finally out on to the terrace. "It's similar to a Frank Lloyd Wright technique: for the sake of drama, you create a pressurized space, then you are released by the wider landscape."

The sunken, enclosed entrance courtyard is loosely based on the geometric Islamic tradition: four square brick fountains are connected by multi-colored runnels and overhung by flowering crab apple trees. The colored metal fountain interiors are lit at night and glow comfortingly. "I wanted a private space, to lead you down into something secret," Schwartz explains.

The terrace behind the house stretches the width of the building and is decorated with various pieces of high-quality folk-art. The other episodes of the garden are discovered one by one, and seem modest in context. "You can't compete with the landscape here," says Schwartz. "We decided not to try to fight it, but to join it." The roof of the swimming-poolhouse is a simple turf rectangle that juts into space, a surreal gesture that also functions as a croquet lawn. There are several other hidden and enclosed sitting spaces at the sides of the house. From the pool itself, swimmers can view the overwhelming landscape through a notch cut in the perimeter wall.

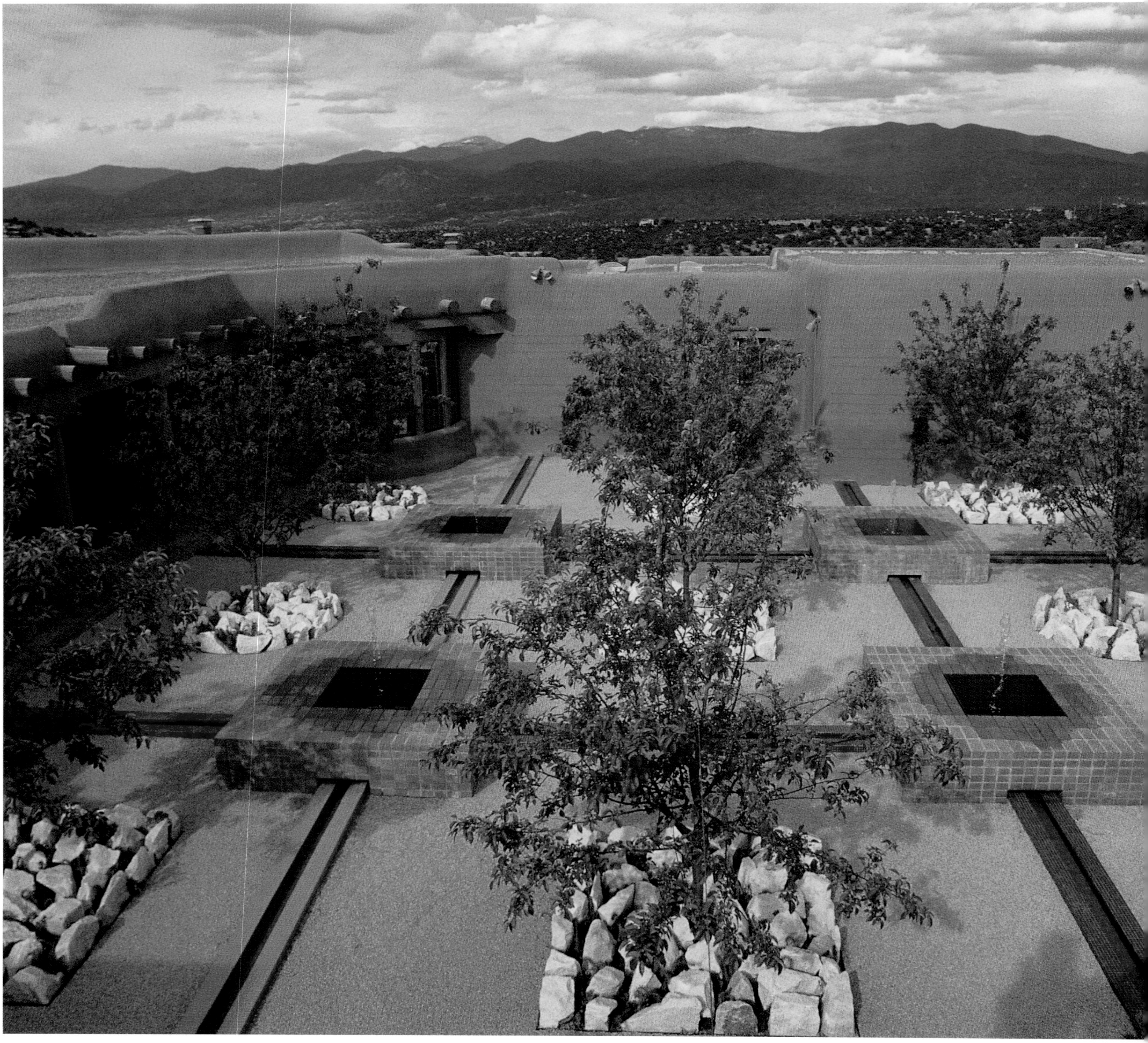

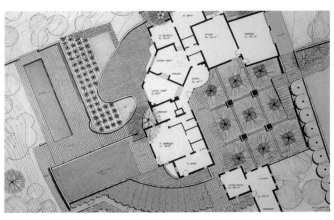

The plan [above] retro-fitted a linear organizational axis that went through the site along with a series of new rooms that re-choreographed the sequential entrance into the house.

The bedroom garden, on top of a newly added poolhouse, was the only place where Schwartz allowed grass. This was the client's "bedroom carpet" and had to feel good underfoot. Schwartz liked the contrast of the lawn – a funky, water-loving and domesticated planting – against the ruggedness of the surrounding high-desert landscape.

Assyria invades the Los Angeles city of commerce

The Citadel

City of Commerce, California   1991
Client: Trammell Crow Company

"An Assyrianoid-esque office park and discount tire center" is how Schwartz describes the extraordinary 1920s zigguratic edifice that was formerly the Uniroyal Tire and Rubber Plant – a landmark in the City of Commerce in Los Angeles. The heart of Schwartz's design is a 700-feet-long entrance drive with the character of a pedestrianized plaza, made up of an austere and impressive grid of date palms, their trunks surrounded by rings of white-painted concrete (a nod to the building's history as a tire factory).

"I wanted to make a great showcase, an entrance worthy of Cleopatra. I wanted it to look like Elizabeth Taylor would go shopping there," Schwartz says. "So we took the service drive and made it into a grand allée as a context for the fancy Assyrian building. It was a private road, which was important, because that meant we didn't

have to do the regulation kerbs or planting strips on sidewalks. The idea was to eliminate the street language and make a European-style plaza: cars drive over it, but it's really for people walking. The big concrete tires round the palms make the roadway and also provide seats. It was a super-simple idea."

The checkerboard paving is composed of a series of colored concrete rectangular pavers. A retail court off the plaza recreates a Middle Eastern bazaar – a space of shade trees and paths, awnings and water. A formal allée of flowering trees connects the central space to a planned hotel. Parking areas are designed to recall the agricultural groves of Southern California and the Mediterranean. Row plantings of dry, greyish olive trees contrast dramatically against the green palm oasis.

The plan has a main ceremonial axis that leads to the building. The parking lot and office buildings flank the axis, while a wholesale shopping mall creates a cross-axis.

Glass-reinforced concrete "tires" ring the bottom of the date palms, creating incidental seating. They also delineate the traffic on a pedestrian oriented plaza.

169

an urban parterre makes for the ultimate park **bench**

Jacob Javits Plaza

New York City, New York 1996
Client: US General Services Administration

In 1992, the Federal Government undertook the repair of the waterproofing for the underground garage beneath the Jacob Javits Plaza in Manhattan. Because the existing plaza would be demolished during the waterproofing construction, the opportunity was taken to revitalize the plaza. During the time that Richard Serra's *Tilted Arc* inhabited the space, the 14-feet-high, 120-feet-long "steel blade" sculpture was widely viewed as an obstruction to pedestrians both visually and physically.

"The Serra was on a heroic scale, but not a human scale," is Schwartz's view. "The buildings round that plaza are horrible, so you had to feel sorry for the people in there who just wanted to go out and have a sandwich. I thought, why should art be above life? That piece focused too much bad energy. Public art does have a role, but the public has to like it. And the people spoke." The realization that there should be a parity between utility and art in public landscape was a defining moment in Schwartz's career.

After the sculpture was removed in 1989, the plaza remained vacant and disconnected from its context. Schwartz's solution was to provide a practical, lively and pleasant seating space for local workers and passers-by, and to reintegrate the plaza with the New York street scene.

The new plaza provides various seating opportunities for people having lunch or just for watching other people. "It's the ultimate park bench," Schwartz says. "It's a *parterre de broderie* made out of looping strands of back-to-back New York City park benches. And it has multiple social possibilities for small or large groups. You can sit in intimate circles or be more spread out. If you are alone, you can sit on the outside curves and not have anyone in your face. And as the seasons change, the shadows move across the plaza, so there is seating everywhere, to follow the seasons."

As in a 17th-century *parterre de broderie*, the complex, swirling forms and bright green, reflective color of the benches energize the flat plane of the plaza. And the topiary forms of a French parterre are echoed in this urban plaza by 6-feet-tall grassy hemispheres that exude mist on hot days and are lit green at night – Schwartz calls them "small centers of visual gravity around which the swirls of benches seem to circle."

But the big structural move was to take out the planters that were placed at two corners of the plaza, plus the long, empty fountain pool that occupied the only sunny portion of the site. "With them in there, you couldn't see the street," Schwartz says. "Now, people can again be part of the street scene." Mutated versions of standard New York park furniture – enameled drinking fountains (bright blue here), wire-mesh trashcans (vivid orange), oversized Central Park lighting standards, concrete bollards (dome-headed), the long benches themselves – are a comment on the overarching presence of Frederick Law Olmsted, designer of Central Park, in the city's landscape tradition. They have been "tweaked," Schwartz says, to offer a wry commentary on the fact that while New York remains a cultural mecca for most art forms, exploration in landscape architecture receives little support.

Of all the projects of Martha Schwartz, Inc. the high-profile Jacob Javits Plaza has attracted most criticism for build quality, and since this attack has been leveled at several of the firm's projects, it needs tackling head on. Schwartz does not deny that many of her landscape projects have a limited life expectancy, but she is unrepentant:

"One of our big problems is, how do we make something out of junk? Clients generally want something quick and cheap. My culture, in the United States, is not a culture of longevity (in Europe, I find they think about how things will weather; they take more care). So we just go ahead, and then we get flak when it falls apart. A lot of my pieces are temporary, or slow-temporary: they might last for 10 years, but not more. But it is a reflection of the budgetary constraints placed on us. Because of a lack of money, some of the materials have a limited lifespan. If you want something to last, you need stronger materials, and they are more expensive. Things like concrete pavers won't last – they fall apart, they crack, they fade, they get brittle. When you build your landscape out of junk, that's what you get. What am I supposed to do – march off the set? No: you see what you can do. If you can transform a space for the public for one second, that's better than not at all. I like to have a moment of glory. Plus, the spaces we design tend to get overused. They get ripped apart and worn down, and there are often maintenance problems. But perhaps if people really like it, they will find ways of maintaining it. You have to inspire advocacy for your landscapes."

After Serra's *Tilted Arc* was removed, the workers in the buildings overwhelmingly asked for a space with lots of seating and trees. Trees were impossible to include due to severe weight limitations. Instead, Schwartz made the ultimate seating plan for a plaza. The winding lines are double rows of continuous benches that flow throughout the plaza.

Although completely dissimilar to Olmsted in plan and concept, the language is all Olmstedian. Schwartz claims that any other design language in New York City is unacceptable.

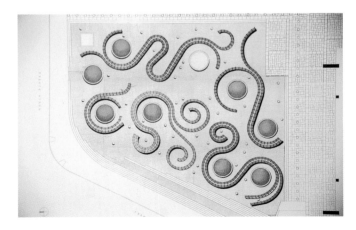

174

Green grass mounds, constructed of lightweight materials, dot the space, providing a subdivision of space when you sit down.

mounds **swim** like whales through a Japanese car park

Nexus Kashi III Housing Project

Fukuoka, Japan   1997
Client: Fukuoka Jisho Co Ltd

In this project, the final phase of a housing development that included six apartment buildings – designed by Mark Mack, OMA/Rem Koolhaas, Steven Holl, Oscar Tusquets, Christian De Portzamparc, and Oshamu Ishiyamu – Martha Schwartz, Inc. was called in to design the public spaces between the buildings.

"We were the last people to be involved," says Schwartz. "By the time we got there, the space was all chopped up. It was like someone had cut out a dress from a pattern on cloth and handed us the remainder. It's hard to create spatial integrity from leftover spaces."

But Schwartz knew she was working in a culture that appreciated exterior design. "People in Japan might not want to participate in gardening – but they want a garden. They want a relief space. In Japan there are always little pieces of gardens – even outside a bathroom there might be a little 2-by-4-foot space.

"But then it turned out that what was really wanted was parking. Clearly even the Japanese valued parking above gardens or landscape. But this outdoor space was also the area that everyone looked at from above, so it had to be experientially interesting."

The solution was to incorporate sculptural mounds – which Schwartz calls "whales" – that lend a sense of movement through the idea of swimming, and help the spaces read as a unity. The grass and stone mounds swim mysteriously through the filtered canopy and vertical trunks of a bamboo forest. "They also take your mind off the shape of the space," Schwartz adds.

Parking spaces for 241 cars and 450 bicycles had to be accommodated, and the resulting expanse of asphalt was enlivened by a series of bright orange discs across the parking spaces. When the majority of the vehicles have disappeared for the working day, lines of majestic palm trees help transform a car park into a distinctive plaza. Repetition is a key visual technique in Schwartz's work. "It is a very good method of lending structure where there is none otherwise – which is often the case," she explains. "The landscape is unstructured space. Nature is not a blank canvas: the basic form outside is visual chaos, and structure and repetition contrasts with that."

The "moving" objects were a strategy to unite a site plan where the spaces had been badly chopped up and had no continuity. The whales were made of stone and grass and swam through a sea of bamboo.

A water whale is made of roof tiles so that water runs off the spine.

A space that was once to be a community garden was turned into a parking lot through tenant demand. Schwartz tried to make the parking attractive to look at by using bold graphics to designate parking space.

A parking lot is transformed into a "place" by using paint.

traffic management (human and vehicular)

Theme Park East Entry Esplanade
Anaheim, California 1998
Client: Disneyland

"At Disneyland we were given a traffic problem," Schwartz explains. "This is the bus entrance to the park, and we needed to make it workable, safe and attractive. So we took the basic language of the highway – steel, cones, asphalt, road markings, walkways, streetlights, traffic lights – and made an exaggerated, multi-colored environment based on that language. We call it a Hyper Highway, because everything is bigger, unreal. As a landscape, it was more or less painted on. The only non-utilitarian aspect of this project is that everything needs repainting regularly."

Shuttle buses from nearby hotels drop off and pick up passengers along linear stopping places. These glorified traffic islands are marked by an insistent and oversized pattern of cross-walks to indicate pedestrian access to the theme-park entrance. Every traffic island is flanked by formal rows of highway lighting standards with a metallic finish, each glowing a different color. The bright light provides not only a dazzling field of color at night, but also helps with the orientation of the traffic – both vehicular and pedestrian.

Reinforced-concrete bollards are shaped as oversized traffic cones, painted green. At one perimeter, a single line of bollards occupies a 5-feet (1.5-meters) wide strip of bright yellow "detectable warning" tile. The tile provides a visual and tactile separation between pedestrians and vehicles. The green cones are also a homage to 17th-century topiaries. Indeed, the overall scheme was inspired by the management and direction of the visitors in French Baroque gardens – an intention that becomes clear when the design is viewed in plan.

182

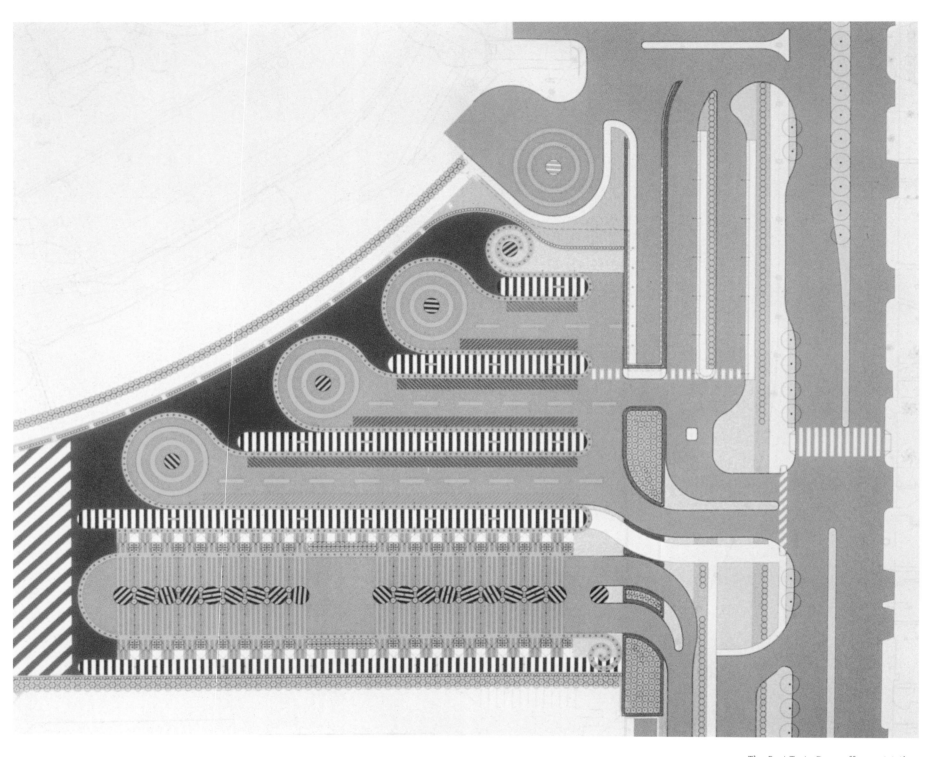

The East Train Drop-off was strictly a
functional area eleven million visitors pass
through to go to Disneyland each year. The
plan is realized using only highway color
codings and design elements.
The design is simplified through repetition,
seriality and color – all Schwartz trademarks.

Cobra-head lights, traffic cones and black and white pedestrian-crossings construct a formal entry allée, while a "Mickey Bench" [above] is a place from which to watch those entering the park.

fairy-tale spaces create stories for buildings

Paul Lincke Höfe

Berlin, Germany 2000
Client: Realprojekt Bau und Boden AG; associated landscape architect: Büro Kiefer

The Brothers Grimm fairy tales are the inspiration for five courtyard gardens in an abandoned telephone factory that has been converted into luxury loft apartments. Situated over a parking garage and in the shadow of surrounding buildings, the courtyards are a series of magical, manmade vignettes. By transforming traditional tales into a built environment, a cultural connection is made with German folklore, through fanciful "make-believe" landscapes. Because the six-story buildings surrounding the courtyards block the sun, the bright, colorful gardens enliven the space and provide a sense of identity for the residents in each of the building's five sections.

"Until recently, landscape design has been pretty didactic in Germany," Schwartz says. "Designers have embraced an aesthetic that expresses ecological process, where nature is assumed to be the politically correct topic for a landscape to explore. These eco-led narratives tend to marginalize cultural issues that may inform design, often resulting in spaces that are ungainly and not particularly exciting or useful to people. Eco-led narrative, eco-revelatory design and eco-aesthetics have been extremely popular approaches for designers. Even though this approach is a good sell, it glosses over the fact that we are building our landscapes and our environment, and that the landscape is a cultural artifact. As such, the landscape is open to our human shaping and interpretation, and

therefore can express many other narratives and have many other expressions, just as sculpture, painting, film and architecture can have infinite topics and an infinite range of aesthetics. Therefore, even though many people believe that a landscape must speak of nature and ecology, I feel the potential for landscape is much wider as a cultural art form. A garden is not merely a plant display.

"The Paul Lincke Höfe is a series of garden spaces where one can be removed from the everyday world and engage in thought, meditation or relaxation: it's a mental space. In these fairy-tale gardens I was trying to make the point that a landscape doesn't have to be about ecology or natural process: it can have a cultural logic. In this case, the gardens tell stories based on Grimms' fairy tales, as opposed to some vague story about ecological reclamation."

Each garden's unique character is accentuated by playful architectural elements, imaginative plantings, and sculptural grade changes. Vertical elements extend the gardens skyward, filling the void between the buildings. Five fairy tales are told through the gardens: The Water Nixie, How Six Made Their Way in the World, The Twelve Brothers, The Juniper Tree, and The Moon. "It doesn't matter if people don't know the specific allegories and symbols in my work," says Schwartz. "It has to stand up by itself. But in this case, each space has a little plaque that tells the story, if one is interested."

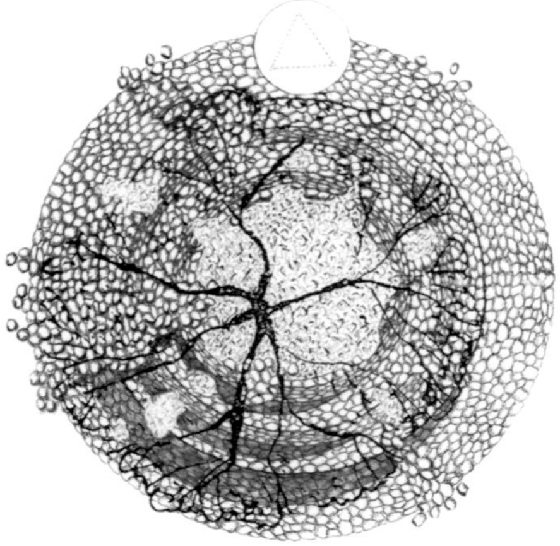

OAK TREE

PLANTER HEIGHT: 1,30 M

RIVER STONES, DIAM. 20 CM +/-
DARK GRAY

PAVING WIDTH:
1,20 M

DIAM. PLANTER: 6,70 M

PAVING WIDTH:
1,20 M

One of five fairy-tale gardens, this one depicts how the moon is in the heavens. Five fiber-glass "moons" raised on steel trusses float above an "ancient" oak grove.

1/2 HOW SIX MADE THEIR WAY IN THE WORLD

This plan [above] depicts how six made their way in the world. It is basically a red and black scheme, depicting a scene where the six brothers find themselves roasting in hell.

190

1/2 THE TWELVE BROTHERS

This plan [above] is the story of the 12 brothers and contains the beds in which they slept. Hanging in the space are the "knitted shirts" made of mesh, which transformed the enchanted boys from swans back into boys.

This garden depicts the story of children pursued by a witch. When they threw things at her, such as their combs, brushes and mirrors, they magically turned into mountains that created obstacles for the witch and helped them escape. These "mountains" became play objects for children to climb on and play in.

a question of **taste**, monumentally posed

51 Garden Ornaments

Schloss Wendlinghausen, Westphalia, Germany   2001
Client: Ministerium für Städtebau und Wohnen Kultur und Sport des Landes Nordrhein-Westfalen

"51 Garden Ornaments," says Schwartz in a written statement, "displays the ornaments that Americans and Germans often choose to place in their gardens. The ornaments have been purchased at garden-store chains that sell high volumes of these artifacts. I have chosen ornaments that also seem most popular and typical. Because of the sheer numbers and ubiquity, these ornaments therefore reflect who we are and how we would like to be seen. They come to characterize a larger collective landscape, as we see them often in each other's yards."

The site for the temporary installation was an old and overgrown garden woodland on a country estate in Germany. Schwartz was instructed that nothing could be permanently changed in this garden, and no major planting or grading of the earth was possible. The installation had to be a light intervention in the landscape. The garden had a rolling, unstructured ground plane and was studded with large, very old trees in no particular pattern or order. To bring order and contrast to the helter-skelter quality of the site, Schwartz's first move was to instruct the ground crew to mow a grid into the field of grass over the course of the spring. These mown pathways created a zig-zag path system for visitors. At the intersections of the pathways, the garden ornaments were placed on plain white bases. Because each garden ornament was not itself particularly striking in the landscape, the bases for the objects did the visual work by imposing pattern within the landscape.

As Schwartz says: "There was a strong spatial structure and a polemic within it. The piece is funny...and critical. The curator, delighted by the high turn-out for the piece, said to me, 'You're a really angry person,' and he was right. There is a strong bite to it, but most people were oblivious to it." As with other Schwartz works, the piece can be understood on several levels. "If people don't want to get it or deal with my anger, they can roam through it and that's fine," Schwartz says. "But for people thinking conceptually, there's something there to reflect upon. My contention is that these ornaments are all things that we put into our gardens. We shopped at these huge garden emporiums in both countries – they are obviously selling this stuff at a great rate and it's pouring out into our suburbs and countryside. To many of us these objects seem low-level and crass, but the process and its results are democratic. People choose these objects to express themselves to their neighbors and to the public at large. There's an ambivalence in my mind as to whether this is good or bad. Perhaps it's both."

There is the difficult question of whether Schwartz is merely satirizing popular taste from a lofty artistic position. Her response: "The answer is yes. It's a great thing that people have choice, as reflected in the huge array of ornaments for sale, and what is placed in the gardens, but it's also true that choice without knowledge or education can be dangerous. Our populace is very undertrained in and underexposed to aesthetics. People believe that having an opinion about art and design is the same as having knowledge about it. But how can people be educated in aesthetics when it's not taught in schools, nor evident in the environment? In the United States the degradation of our visual environment is happening at a much greater rate than elsewhere, perhaps because of the great choice we have in materials. My criticism is that this lack of aesthetic awareness in our environment is ultimately not going to add up to anything good."

The installation is in an old Schloss garden that could not be touched or permanently altered. The scheme involved creating a point grid of large white boxes (that served as pedestals) upon a grid mown in the grass.

The objects of "low culture" were displayed
on the white boxes, as in a museum. The
lawn jockey, tire with geraniums and the
wishing well are American favorites.

These ornaments are tremendously popular with the public in both Germany and the US. What does this say about us? It is a democratic process of design in which people have choice, and exercise it. Millions of dollars worth of these objects are sold every year.

color-coded **interior** spaces define an office building

Swiss Re Headquarters

Munich, Germany 2002

Client: Swiss Re; architect: BRT Architekten; associated landscape architect: Peter Kluska Landschaftsarchitekt

The landscape surrounding a new office headquarters for a German insurance company divides the site into four quadrants, each assigned a different color: red, blue, yellow, green. Each quadrant is made up of strips of plants, hard materials and sculptural objects that radiate out from the building. A pool, also divided into colored quadrants, creates a tranquil spot at the center of the building; one quadrant is filled with water lilies, and just beneath the still surface are vibrantly colored gazing globes, marbles, crushed glass, gravel and terracotta pots. The whole building is encircled by a vine-covered walkway, or floating hedge, at the level of the third story.

"This is a corporation where they have an interest in the employees' quality of life," Schwartz says. "They have a good chef who cooks everyone delicious and healthy meals. On this project, the landscape was not an afterthought. The building is sited in an office-park-no-man's-land near Munich airport. The company was one of the first kids on the block, and they wanted something quite inward-looking. The concept of the building was to create an internalized space with views to gardens."

There were serious practical problems to overcome, however. Every "landscape" surface of the building was on top of its structure, so lightweight materials had to be used. Many of the garden spaces were in permanent shade. And there was little soil to work with so smaller plants had to be used. "We never met earth," Schwartz says. "It was a little like doing gardens on a spaceship. Given the situation, we had to use materials other than plants to make these spaces interesting. The Germans love plants and are almost phobic about using inorganic materials, so we used non-living organic materials." The idea of the strips came from the fact that the office park had been built on top of agricultural fields – the gardens were like miniature ploughed fields – and the color coding and distinctive garden themes were intended to aid orientation and create identity within the building.

The graphic nature of this design is a reflection of Schwartz's training as a printmaker and is the product of a working method that developed from that background. "I draw designs out on paper first," she says. "I start with a graphic depiction of space and work up from there, from 2-D to 3-D. I always start off in plan – that organizes my ideas, because when you go to visit these sites, their size can seem overwhelming. Often when I come back, I feel overwhelmed by the space; it seems impossible, chaotic. The only way to deal with it is to reduce it to plan form and compose from that. To make something read in the landscape, which is inherently chaotic, you need something strong and simple at the core. But, typically, you have to get beyond the graphic and into the sculpture/spatial realm to make it work. You can't work too delicately in the landscape – you have to have something fundamentally stronger and more cohesive than the context in order to hold it together. My intention is to create something that can be seen through contrast with a chaotic environment."

The plan is based on the division of the building into four quadrants, each with its own color. The design recalls the structure of the agricultural field that the building replaced.

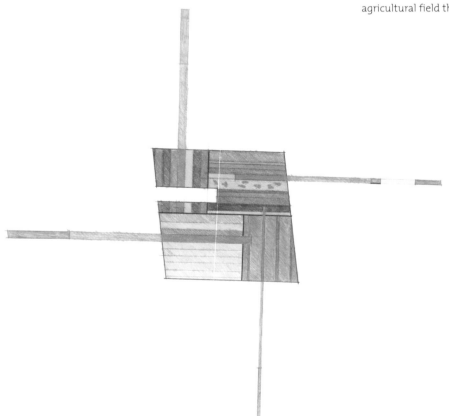

"Technical materials," or non-plants were used in the many shaded areas where plants couldn't grow. All these materials – green glass in stainless-steel boxes, red-dyed logs, blue stacks of glass and yellow sandstones – converge at the central water garden. The building is spatially complex. The mirrored balls were used in spaces under the offices in order to add life, sparkle and light in otherwise perpetually shaded areas.

The striated fields were applied to all surfaces including the roofs, the terrace and the groundplane. Because of the complexity of the structure, the color becomes instrumental in orientating oneself when inside.

fish link the railway to the river

Lehrter Bahnhof Berlin

Berlin, Germany   2004
Client: Deutsche Bahn AG, City of Berlin

In February 1999, Martha Schwartz, in association with Büro Kiefer of Berlin, won first place in the Lehrter Bahnhof Competition that called for the design of a plaza for the new railway station in Berlin, Germany. As the focus of the modern traffic system in Berlin, in Schwartz's view the station is a symbol of a society preoccupied by speed and movement. Located at the convergence of various transportation systems, urban districts, and scales, the site is complex, with conflicting claims on its use.

As designed by Schwartz, the plaza provides a spatial connection between the two large structures that characterize Berlin's urban space: the River Spree, which runs through a concrete channel, and the elevated train tracks. The plaza provides a transition between the open landscape of the Tiergarten to the south and the densely built city. The design aims to create a coherent space with the power to resolve the site's complex changes in elevations and technical requirements, with the potential to become a culturally significant landmark of Berlin.

The heart of the design is a linear fish tank filled with fish from the River Spree. Measuring 80 meters (262 feet) long, 2 meters (6½ feet) high, and 5 meters (16½ feet) wide, the fish tank begins at the station and projects out to the River Spree. "The fish swimming in the tank enrich the plaza with an attractive irony," Schwartz says. "Even when the plaza is empty, there is life." At the end of the fish tank near the River Spree, it takes on the character of a billboard and provides current information about the actual condition of the River Spree water. The river, long denied in the consciousness of the city, is given new importance as a feature in the center of Berlin.

The other elements of the plaza are trees, benches, and stairs. The west side of the plaza has a compact planting of three rows of weeping willows and benches that connect the street trees in the blocks west of the plaza with the riverbank vegetation of the Spree. On the east side of the plaza, wooden benches, reminiscent of railroad ties, are placed comb-like at right angles to the facade. To the south and west, the plaza and the street levels are connected by generous stairways. To accentuate the changes in the site's topography, the area of the plaza that extends from the station hall toward the River Spree is raised slightly. The south-west tip of this platform rises over the street level terminating in a landing with views to the Spree, the Spreebogenpark, the government quarter, and the Tiergarten. Completion is slated for 2004.

Competition drawings showing plans and elevations of the minimalist plaza with the fish tank that connects the train station to the river.

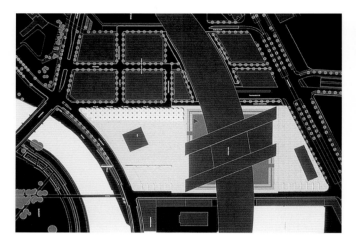

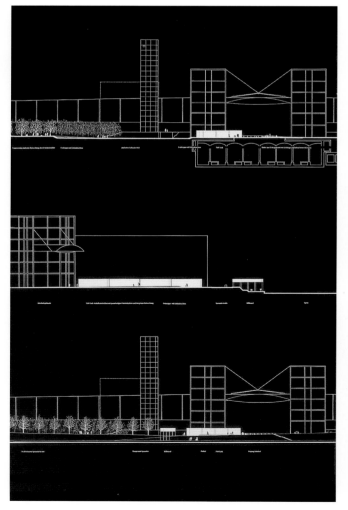

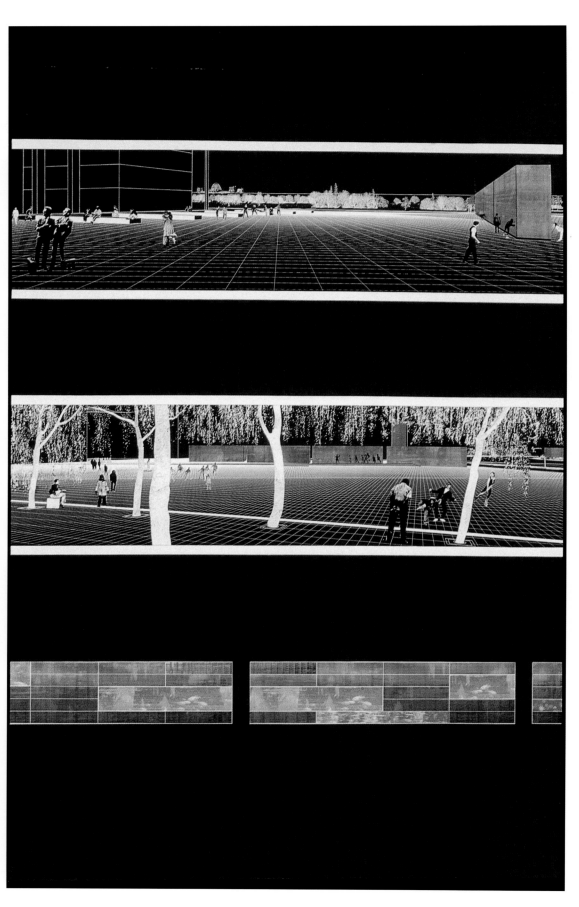

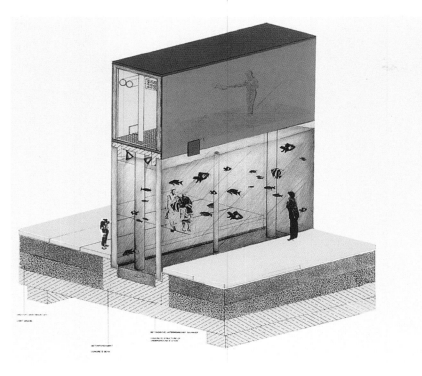

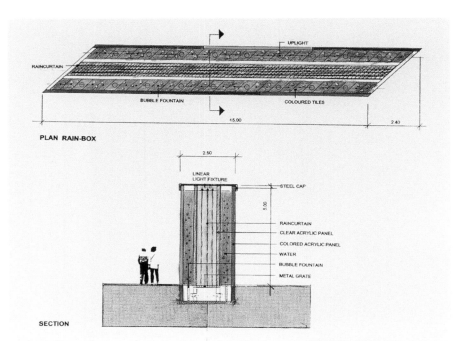

PLAN RAIN-BOX

SECTION

DETAIL: RAIN-BOX M: 1:50
Datum: 07. 03. 2001

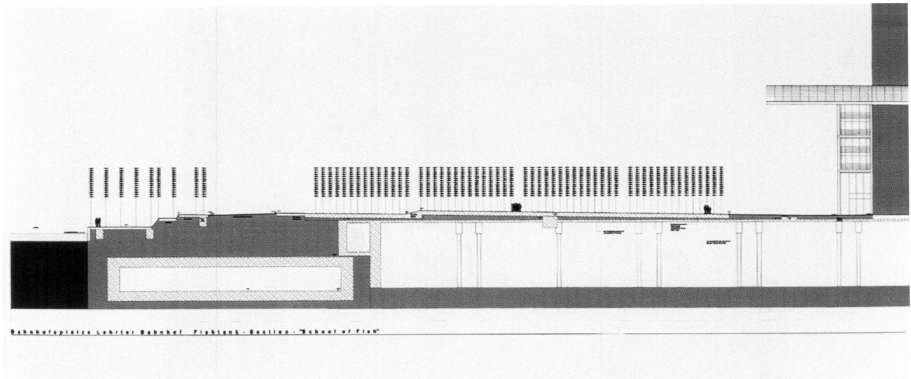

Technical sections through different "fish tank" possibilities. A section through the clear acrylic tank [top left] shows columns supporting the structure of two tubes: a lower one for the fish, an upper one for maintenance. A variation [top right] shows the tank as a fountain made of colored acrylic and lights. A section through the entire structure [bottom] illustrates the train tunnel and a wind sculpture made of thousands of fish weather vanes.

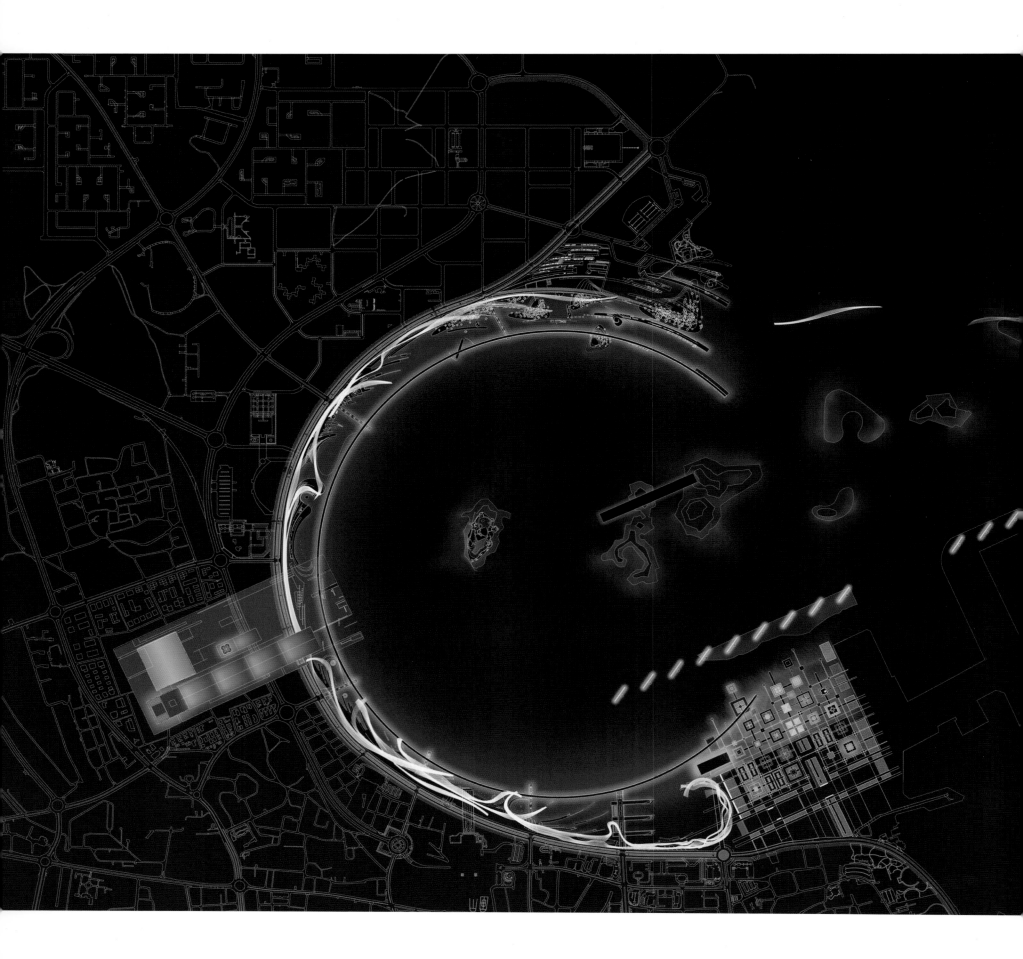

the **life** of people and plants usurps the rule of the automobile

Doha Corniche

Doha, Qatar   2003

Clients: Center for Arts & Culture, National Council for Culture, Arts and Heritage, The State of Qatar, The Aga Khan Trust for Culture

Schwartz's plan for revitalizing the 4½-miles (7.5-kilometers) long corniche road of Doha and its environs is based on the idea of four concentric "C" zones along the promenade edge. The first is the corniche road itself; the second the promenade at the waterside; the third a new eco-zone between the promenade and the fourth zone, the boardwalk, a floating structure accessible by water taxi. The disparate elements of the scheme will be linked by eight walking loops, each with its own character.

"The task of making a corniche is particularly interesting," Schwartz says. "The word itself is associated with some of the most beautiful and romantic areas of the world: Cannes, Monaco, the Italian Riviera. This image is idealized by beautiful coastal scenery, and a sense of movement and passage. It is a place where people and automobiles come together. It is a place of hustle and bustle, of people 'making the scene', coming and going, seeing and being seen."

The corniche road will be embedded into the city life by the introduction of measures for slowing and reducing traffic (through tree planting) to create a sense of promenade, and by encouraging smaller shops and restaurants into the zone.

The waterside promenade will be a sinuous movement of golden stone pathways that create a highly articulated and sculptural edge. Its serrations become ramps, steps, seating, walkways, beaches, docks, breakwaters, and animal habitats. Along the promenade, will be restaurants, mosques, bookshops, playgrounds, stages and fountains. Above it will float the "White Necklace," a curvy white trellis structure that will flow along the length of the corniche and vary in height and width, casting intricate shadows and lighting up at night. "This work of art evokes memories of a landscape of a nomadic heritage," Schwartz says. "Billowing tents, flowing abaya, and the ongoing celebration of the desert landscape's powerful horizontality."

The ecological element of the plan reintroduces the black mangrove and marsh grasses (with the attendant waterfowl) to the Doha waterfront and the aquatic subsoils to facilitate their growth. The floating boardwalk provides views back to Doha and the setting for three substantial parks, Mangrove Park, Central Park and Museum Park, the latter to include a botanical greenhouse, formal gardens, a butterfly house, swimming atoll and aviaries, all sited around the existing museums.

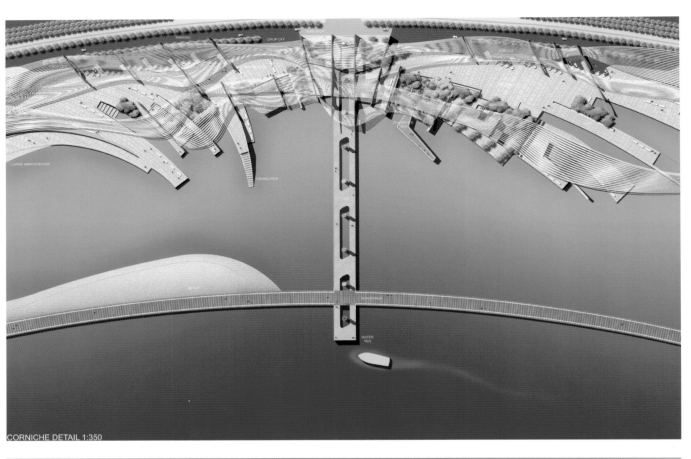

A bird's-eye view of the "White Necklace" trellis structure that floats above the surface of the promenade [above].

A detailed plan of the promenade [right] illustrating a highly articulated edge for activities, including the trellis and a pier that connects the promenade to the new boardwalk and spans a new "Eco-Zone."

CORNICHE DETAIL 1:350

A bird's-eye view of the Museum Park [right], a people's park where I. M. Pei's Museum of Cultural Heritage is being built. The gardens are based on the structure of an Islamic garden. A formal structure and pattern contain different activities and programs: greenhouses, restaurants, an aviary, "coolhouses," swimming holes, fountains, parking and other museums.

A plan of the Mangrove Park [opposite above], shows the inter-tidal park created for the restoration of Doha's native habitat.

Sections through the promenade [opposite center] showing the corniche road, the tram system, trellis and pier and the Museum Park [opposite bottom] with floating islands and dense cypress walls.

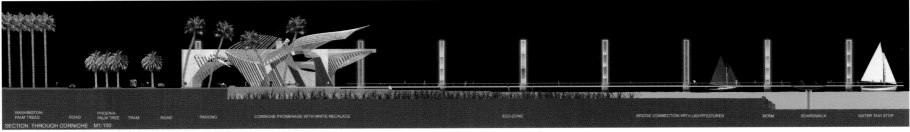

SECTION THROUGH CORNICHE M1:100

WASHINGTON-PALM TREES ROAD PHOENIX-PALM TREE TRAM ROAD PARKING CORNICHE PROMENADE WITH WHITE NECKLACE ECO-ZONE BRIDGE CONNECTION WITH LIGHTFEATURES BERM BOARDWALK WATER TAXI STOP

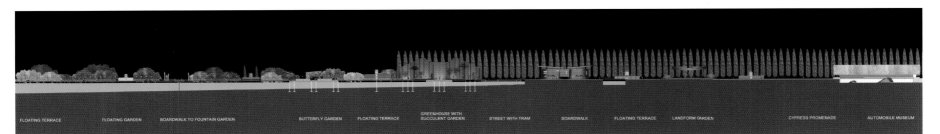

FLOATING TERRACE FLOATING GARDEN BOARDWALK TO FOUNTAIN GARDEN BUTTERFLY GARDEN FLOATING TERRACE GREENHOUSE WITH SUCCULENT GARDEN STREET WITH TRAM BOARDWALK FLOATING TERRACE LANDFORM GARDEN CYPRESS PROMENADE AUTOMOBILE MUSEUM

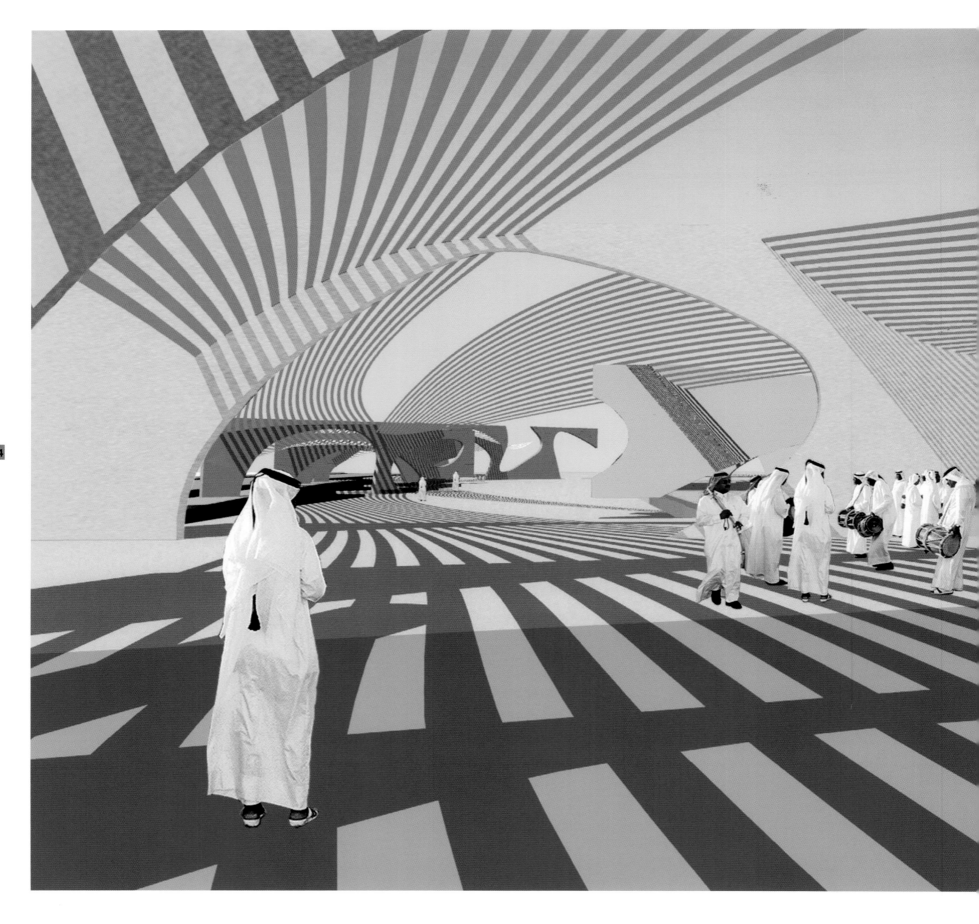

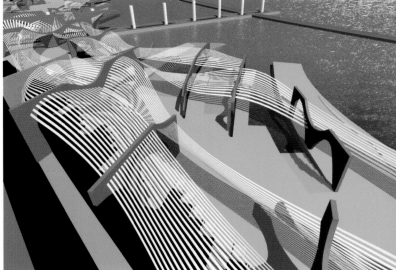

215

Computer renderings illustrate the quality of the space and light under the "White Necklace" trellis. The structure, made of aluminum tubes and concrete walls, provides a much-needed identity for the corniche and ameliorates the heat by creating shade. The shadow patterns create a fantastic, dynamic daytime environment using the climate's sun and strong shadows and will be illuminated at night. In heavily used areas the structure also contains a misting system.

Complete Projects

Necco Garden

Splice Garden

Texas Bluebonnet Garden

Rio Shopping Center

Bagel Garden
Cambridge, Massachusetts
1979
Martha Schwartz

Necco Garden
Cambridge, Massachusetts
1980
Martha Schwartz, Peter Walker,
Rebecca Schwartz

Stella Garden
Bala-Cynwyd, Pennsylvania
1980
Martha Schwartz

Puerto de Europa
Madrid, Spain
1985
Schwartz Smith Meyer Landscape Architects:
Martha Schwartz, Ken Smith, David Meyer

Whitehead Institute Splice Garden
Cambridge, Massachusetts
1986
The Office of Peter Walker
and Martha Schwartz:
Martha Schwartz, Bradley Burke

Morgan Residence
Los Angeles, California
1986
Martha Schwartz, Inc:
Martha Schwartz
Associated Landscape Architect: Mia Lehrer

International Swimming Hall of Fame
Fort Lauderdale, Florida
1987
The Office of Peter Walker
and Martha Schwartz:
Martha Schwartz,
Ken Smith, Gabe Ruspini
Architect: Arquitectonica International

King County Jailhouse Garden
Seattle, Washington
1987
The Office of Peter Walker
and Martha Schwartz:
Martha Schwartz, Ken Smith,
Martin Poirier, Bradley Burke

Texas Bluebonnet Garden
Austin Airport, Texas
1988
Schwartz Smith Meyer Landscape Architects:
Martha Schwartz, Ken Smith, David Meyer

Center for Innovative Technology
Fairfax, Virginia
1988
The Office of Peter Walker
and Martha Schwartz:
Martha Schwartz, Ken Smith, David Meyer,
Martin Poirier
Architect: Arquitectonica International

Limed Parterre with Skywriter
Cambridge, Massachusetts
1988
The Office of Peter Walker
and Martha Schwartz:
Martha Schwartz, Ken Smith

Rio Shopping Center
Atlanta, Georgia
1988
The Office of Peter Walker
and Martha Schwartz:
Ken Smith, David Meyer, Martin Poirier,
Doug Findlay, David Walker
Architect: Arquitectonica International

Turf Parterre Garden
New York City, New York
1988
The Office of Peter Walker
and Martha Schwartz:
Martha Schwartz, Ken Smith

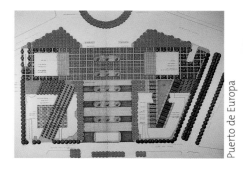
Puerto de Europa

International Swimming Hall of Fame

Center for Innovative Technology

Turf Parterre Garden

Becton Dickinson

Villamoura, Portugal

Snoopy's Garden

Cumberland Park

Becton Dickinson
San Jose, California
1990
Schwartz Smith Meyer Landscape Architects:
Martha Schwartz, Ken Smith, David Meyer,
Doug Findlay, David Jung, Sara Fairchild
Architect: Gensler and Associates

Kunsthal Museumpark
Rotterdam, The Netherlands
1990
Schwartz Smith Meyer Landscape Architects:
Martha Schwartz, Ken Smith, David Meyer
Architect: Rem Koolhaas

Moscone Center
San Francisco, California
1990
Schwartz Smith Meyer Landscape Architects:
Martha Schwartz, Ken Smith, Sara Fairchild

Villamoura
Algarve, Portugal
1990
Schwartz Smith Meyer Landscape Architects:
Martha Schwartz, Ken Smith, David Meyer
Architects: Arquitectonica International

The Citadel
City of Commerce, Los Angeles, California
1991
Schwartz Smith Meyer Landscape Architects:
Ken Smith, David Meyer, Sara Fairchild,
Kathryn Drinkhouse
Architect: The Nadel Partnership

Dickenson Residence
Santa Fe, New Mexico
1991
Schwartz Smith Meyer Landscape Architects:
Martha Schwartz, David Meyer,
Sara Fairchild, Ken Smith
Architect: Steven Jacobson

Snoopy's Garden
Ito, Japan
1991
Schwartz Smith Meyer Landscape Architects:
Martha Schwartz, Ken Smith, David Meyer
Architects: Philip Johnson, John Burgee

Jazz Hall of Fame
Kansas City, Missouri
Conception 1992
Schwartz Smith Meyer Landscape Architects:
Martha Schwartz, Ken Smith, David Meyer

Cumberland Park
Toronto, Ontario, Canada
1993
Schwartz Smith Meyer Landscape Architects:
Ken Smith, David Meyer

World Cup
Various locations throughout the US
1994
Martha Schwartz, Inc:
Martha Schwartz, Maria Bellalta, Leo Jew

Baltimore Inner Harbor (competition)
Baltimore, Maryland
1995
Martha Schwartz, Inc:
Martha Schwartz, Maria Bellalta, Leo Jew,
Laura Rutledge, Paula Meijerink, Evelyn
Bergaila, Michael Blier, Chris MacFarlane
Associated Architect: Design Collective, Inc

Delano Hotel
Miami Beach, Florida
1995
Martha Schwartz, Inc:
Martha Schwartz

Littman Wedding
Deal, New Jersey
1995
Martha Schwartz, Inc:
Martha Schwartz, Paula Meijerink,
Kevin Conger

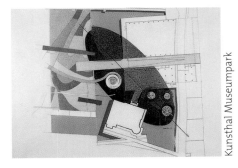
Kunsthal Museumpark

Dickenson Residence

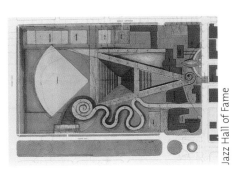
Jazz Hall of Fame

Delano Hotel

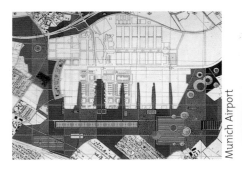
Munich Airport

Miami International Airport

Lincoln Road Mall

Geraldton Mine Project

Munich Airport
Munich, Germany
1995
Martha Schwartz, Inc:
Paula Meijerink, Markus Jatsch,
Kevin Conger, Kaki Martin

Davis Residence
El Paso, Texas
1996
Martha Schwartz, Inc:
Martha Schwartz, Michael Blier, Sara
Fairchild, Kevin Conger, Paula Meijerink

Jacob Javits Plaza
New York City, New York
1996
Martha Schwartz, Inc:
Martha Schwartz, Laura Rutledge, Maria
Bellalta, Chris MacFarlane, Michael Blier,
Leo Jew

**Miami International Airport Sound
Attenuation Wall**
Miami, Florida
1996
Martha Schwartz, Inc:
Martha Schwartz, Kevin Conger,
Sara Fairchild, Chris Macfarlane, Laura
Rutledge, Maria Bellalta, Leo Jew

Winslow Farms Conservancy
Hammonton, New Jersey
1996
Martha Schwartz, Inc:
Martha Schwartz, Kathryn Drinkhouse,
Michael Blier, Kevin Conger, Paula Meijerink

Nexus Kashi III
Fukuoka, Japan
1997
Martha Schwartz, Inc:
Martha Schwartz, Paula Meijerink,
Michael Blier, Chris MacFarlane,
Kevin Conger

Lincoln Road Mall
Miami Beach, Florida
1997
Martha Schwartz, Inc:
Martha Schwartz, Michael Blier,
Paula Meijerink, Chris MacFarlane

Spoleto Festival
Charleston, North Carolina
1997
Martha Schwartz, Inc:
Martha Schwartz, Lisa Delplace, Lital Fabian,
Evelyn Bergaila, Wes Michaels, Kaki Martin,
and others

US Courthouse Plaza
Minneapolis, Minnesota
1997
Martha Schwartz, Inc:
Martha Schwartz, Paula Meijerink, Chris
MacFarlane, Laura Rutledge, Maria Bellalta,
Leo Jew

Broward County Civic Arena
Fort Lauderdale, Florida
1998
Martha Schwartz, Inc:
Martha Schwartz, Donald Sharp,
Tricia Bales, Lital Fabian

Geraldton Mine Project
Geraldton, Ontario, Canada
1998
Martha Schwartz, Inc:
Martha Schwartz, Lital Fabian,
James Lord, Tricia Bales

HUD Plaza Improvements
Washington, DC
1998
Martha Schwartz, Inc:
Martha Schwartz, Evelyn Bergaila, Paula
Meijerink, Chris MacFarlane, Michael Blier,
Kevin Conger, Sara Fairchild, Scott Wunderle,
Kaki Martin, David Bartsch, Rick Casteel
Associated Architect: Architrave, P.C.

Jacob Javits Plaza

Nexus Kashi III

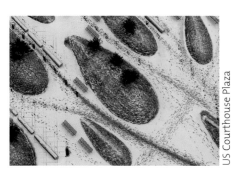
US Courthouse Plaza

HUD Plaza Improvements

Marina Linear Park

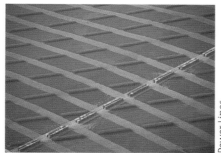
Power Lines

Albuquerque Interstate Corridor

Gifu Kitagata Apartments

Marina Linear Park
San Diego, California
1998
The Office of Peter Walker
and Martha Schwartz

Theme Park Entry Esplanade
Anaheim, California / WDI
1998
Martha Schwartz, Inc:
Martha Schwartz, Donald Sharp,
Paula Meijerink, Lital Fabian, Sari Weissman,
Tricia Bales, Evelyn Bergaila, Scott Carmen,
Shauna Gillies-Smith, Don Sharp,
Jennifer Brooke, Paula Meijerink
Central Plaza: Martha Schwartz, Donald
Sharp, Lital Fabian, Shauna Gillies-Smith,
Paula Meijerink, Tricia Bales, Scott Carmen,
Rafael Justewicz, Michel Langevin,
Wes Michaels, Melanie Mignault

Power Lines
Gelsenkirchen, Germany
1999
Martha Schwartz, Inc:
Martha Schwartz, Markus Jatsch

Winterthur Competition
Winterthur, Switzerland
1999
Martha Schwartz, Inc:
Martha Schwartz, Paula Meijerink,
Wes Michaels, Lital Fabian

Lehrter Bahnhof (competition)
Berlin, Germany
1999–2004
Martha Schwartz, Inc:
Martha Schwartz, Paula Meijerink,
Tricia Bales, Melanie Mignault,
Michael Glueck, Shauna Gillies-Smith,
Mike Kilkelly, France Cormier, Lital Fabian,
Wes Michaels, Kristina Patterson
Associated Landscape Architect:
Büro Kiefer (Berlin)

**Albuquerque Interstate Corridor
Enhancement Plan**
Albuquerque, New Mexico
2000
Martha Schwartz, Inc:
Martha Schwartz, Paula Meijerink,
Tricia Bales, Shauna Gillies-Smith

Denver Airport
Denver, Colorado
2000
Martha Schwartz, Inc:
Martha Schwartz, Jane Choi, Scott Carmen,
Sari Weissman, Isabel Zempel,
Evelyn Bergaila, Steve Foster

Exchange Square
Manchester, UK
2000
Martha Schwartz, Inc:
Martha Schwartz, Shauna Gillies-Smith,
Don Sharp, Paula Meijerink, Lital Fabian,
Tricia Bales, Wes Michaels, Evelyn Bergaila,
Scott Carmen, Rafael Justewicz
Illustrations by Michael Blier

Gifu Kitagata Apartments
Kitagata, Japan
2000
Martha Schwartz, Inc:
Martha Schwartz, Paula Meijerink,
Shauna Gillies-Smith, Michael Blier,
Chris MacFarlane, Kaki Martin, Don Sharp

Paul Lincke Höfe
Berlin, Germany
2000
Martha Schwartz, Inc:
Martha Schwartz, Paula Meijerink,
Patricia Bales, Scott Carmen, Lital Fabian,
Francesca Levaggi, Wes Michaels,
Shauna Gillies-Smith, Michael Wasser,
James Lord
Associated Landscape Architect: Büro
Kiefer (Berlin)

Detmold Redevelopment Plan
Detmold, Germany
Conception 2000
Martha Schwartz, Inc:
Martha Schwartz

Theme Park Entry Esplanade

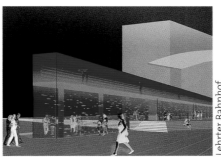
Lehrter Bahnhof

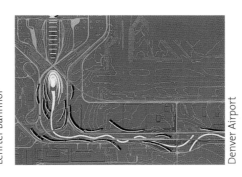
Denver Airport

Paul Lincke Höfe

National Underground Railroad

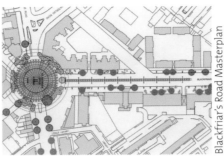

Blackfriar's Road Masterplan

Crawford Museum

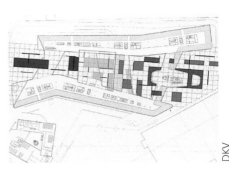

DKV

National Underground Railroad Freedom Center
Cincinnati, Ohio
Conception 2000
Martha Schwartz, Inc:
Martha Schwartz, Shauna Gillies-Smith,
Donald Sharp, Wes Michaels, Tricia Bales,
Paula Meijerink, Lital Szmuk, Sari Weissman,
Ben Kubier, Michael Kilkelly, Michael Glueck,
France Cormier, Krystal England,
Albert Jacob, Letitia Tormay, Nate Trevethan,
Nicole Gaenzler, Steve Foster, Lital Fabian,
Kristina Patterson
Collaboration with Walter Hood

51 Garden Ornaments
Westphalia, Germany
2001
Martha Schwartz, Inc:
Martha Schwartz, Isabel Zempel

Blackfriar's Road Masterplan
London, UK
2001
Martha Schwartz, Inc:
Martha Schwartz, Paula Meijerink,
Nate Trevethan

Bo 01: City of Tomorrow Exhibition
Malmö, Sweden
2001
Martha Schwartz, Inc:
Martha Schwartz, France Cormier

Crawford Museum
Cleveland, Ohio
2001
Martha Schwartz, Inc:
Martha Schwartz, Shauna Gillies-Smith,
Sari Weissman, France Cormier,
Paula Meijerink, Jane Choi

New Mexico Balloon Park
Albuquerque, New Mexico
2001
Martha Schwartz, Inc:
Martha Schwartz, Evelyn Bergaila,
Paula Meijerink, Michael Blier, Lital Fabian,
Kaki Martin, Chris MacFarlane

Bahndeckel Theresienhohe
Munich, Germany
2001
Martha Schwartz, Inc:
Martha Schwartz, Isabel Zempel

Bavarian National Museum Competition
Munich, Germany
2001
Martha Schwartz, Inc:
Martha Schwartz, Isabel Zempel

DKV
Cologne, Germany
Conception 2001
Martha Schwartz, Inc:
Martha Schwartz, Nicole Gaenzler,
Isabel Zempel, Michael Glueck,
Paula Meijerink, Letitia Tormay,
France Cormier, Sari Weissman
Architect: Jan Störmer

Mesa Arts & Entertainment Center
Mesa, Arizona
2001– ongoing
Martha Schwartz, Inc:
Shauna Gillies-Smith, Donald Sharp,
France Cormier, Roy Fabian, Kristina
Patterson, Krystal England, Sari Weissman,
Michael Glueck, Nicole Gaenzler, Lital Szmuk,
Michael Kilkelly, Nate Trevethan, Lital Fabian,
Wes Michaels, Susan Ornelas, Patricia Bales,
Paula Meijerink
Architect: BOORA Architects, Inc.

51 Garden Ornaments

Bo 01: City of Tomorrow exhibition

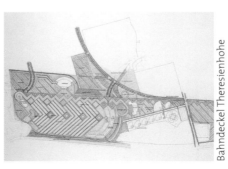

Bahndeckel Theresienhohe

Mesa Arts & Entertainment Center

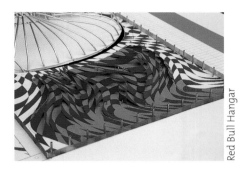
Red Bull Hangar

Spoor Nord Competition

Coventry Civic Squares

Crescent Eastbank Riverside Park

NATO Headquarters
Brussels, Belgium
2002
Martha Schwartz, Inc:
Martha Schwartz, Isabel Zempel

Red Bull Hangar
Salzburg Airport, Austria
2002
Martha Schwartz, Inc:
Martha Schwartz, Isabel Zempel,
France Cormier, Sari Weissman

Spoor Nord Competition
Antwerp, Belgium
2002
Martha Schwartz, Inc:
Martha Schwartz, Isabel Zempel, Jan Bunge
Architect: Neutelings Riedijk Architecten

Swiss Re Headquarters
Munich, Germany
2002
Martha Schwartz, Inc:
Martha Schwartz, Paula Meijerink,
Tricia Bales, Wes Michaels, Michael Langevin,
Melanie Mignault, Shauna Gillies-Smith,
Michael Glueck, Lital Fabian, Krystal England,
Nicole Gaenzler
Architects: BRT Architekten
Associated Landscape Architect: Peter Kluska
Landschaftsarchitekt

Wakefield/Rennie House
London, UK
2002
Martha Schwartz, Inc:
Martha Schwartz, Nate Trevethan
Architect: Wilkinson Eyre

Autoland
Shanghai, China
Conception 2002
Martha Schwartz, Inc:
Martha Schwartz, Isabel Zempel
Architect: Philip Johnson Alan Ritchie
Architects

Coventry Civic Squares
Coventry, UK
Conception 2002
Martha Schwartz, Inc:
Martha Schwartz
Associated Landscape Architect:
Derek Lovejoy Partnership

Wimmer Vienna
Vienna, Austria
Conception 2002
Martha Schwartz, Inc:
Martha Schwartz, Isabel Zempel, France
Cormier, Paula Meijerink, Nicole Gaenzler

Crescent Eastbank Riverside Park
Portland, Oregon
2003
Martha Schwartz, Inc:
Martha Schwartz, Shauna Gillies-Smith,
France Cormier, Sari Weissman,
Paula Meijerink, Donald Sharp,
Nicole Gaenzler, Letitia Tormay
Prime Consultant: OTAK, Inc, Don Hanson,
Kerry Lankford

Doha Corniche
Doha, Qatar
Conception 2003
Martha Schwartz, Inc:
Martha Schwartz, Darren Sears,
Claudia Harari, Donald Booth, Isabel Zempel,
Ramsey Badawi, Nora Libertun,
Lupita Berlanga, Christian Weier,
Hong Zhou, Xun Li

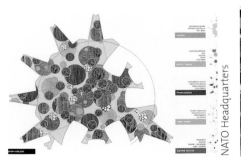
NATO Headquarters

Swiss Re Headquarters

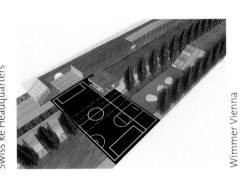
Wimmer Vienna

Doha Corniche

Bibliography

"[Urban] Jungle Warfare," Pamela Young, *Azure*, July/August 2003

"Land Marks: Martha Schwartz talks with Nina James," Nina James, *Architecture Boston*, March/April 2003

Architecture in the Garden, James van Sweden, Random House, New York, 2002

"Martha Schwartz: La Progression de Los Materials," Jeannette Plaut, *Ambientes*, December 2002

"The Willow, Malmö, Sweden," "Mesa Arts and Entertainment Center" and "Exchange Square, Manchester, England," *Dialogue*, August 2002

"Architektur und Natur," *Baumeister, Architektur und Landschaft*, August 2002

"(Dueling Designers) Rooftop Warriors," Carolyn Sollis, *House Beautiful*, July 2002

"Eine Harte Sache," Alexander Hosch, *Architectural Digest – Germany*, June/July 2002

"Martha Schwartz in Full Color," Erika Entholt, *Premium*, April 2002

"Manchester 'Puddingstein', Granit und Stahl," *Garten + Landschaft*, April 2002

"A Constellation of Pieces," Marc Treib, *Landscape Architecture*, March 2002

"Martha Schwartz: Bunte Garten Bilder," Heidi Wiesse, *Eden*, March 2002

"Between the Lines: Designer Profile," Chris Young, *Garden Design Journal*, February/March 2002

"Martha Schwartz, USA, fascinerar med trasslig tårpil," *B001 Framtidsstaden*, August 2001

"In the Public Realm," Keith Franklin West, *Charleston*, May/June 2001

"Avant-Garden," Leslie Forbes, *Gardens Illustrated*, May 2001

"Paul Lincke Höfe," *Land Forum*, No. 6, June 2000

"Garten der vier Jahreszeiten in Japan," *Garten + Landschaft*, April 2001

"Kitagata Garden City," Phoebe Chow, *The Architectural Review*, April 2001

"Martha Schwartz – Exchange Square, Power Lines, Giardini Kitagata," Francesco Repishti (ed.), *Lotus Navigator*, March 2001

"Without Bells and Whistles," Brenda Brown, *Landscape Architecture*, February 2001

"Berlin Von Hinten," Ulrich Timm, *Haüser*, January 2001

"Facelift for the future – Barrick puts a new front on Geraldton," John Martschuk, *Coal Mining Journal*, January 2001

"Martha Schwartz: Making Landscapes Pop," Fred Bernstein, *The New York Times*, 21 December 2000

"Martha Schwartz in Washington," Nora Richter Greer, *de Architect*, November 2000

"Allegro con brio," *Duzaúh*, 2000

"Workstation – Kitagata Apartment Reconstruction Project, the Courtyard Project, Gifu," *Dialogue*, September 2000

"Grootschalige renovatie woningbouw in Gifu: Een opmerkelijk feministisch project in Japan," Paula Meijerink, *Groen*, October 2000

"Anything But Square," Fred Bernstein, *The Sunday Review*, September 2000

"Manchester: 'Pudding-Stein' trifft Granit und Stahl," Martha Schwartz and Shauna Gillies-Smith, *Topos*, September 2000

"Tipps & Trends Garten," Uta Abendroth, *Schöner Wohnen*, June 2000

"America's 10 Most Innovative Gardens," Gordon Taylor and Guy Cooper, *New Eden*, May/June 2000

"What Martha Did in New Mexico," Tim Richardson, *New Eden*, May/June 2000

"Regenerating Landscapes," *New Heritage*, May 2000

"Gärten Der Zukunft," Viola Effmert, *Architekt Wirtschaft Recht*, May 2000

"Gifu Kitagata Apartment," *GA Japan*, May–June 2000

"Gifu Kitagata Apartments Second Phase," *Shinkenchiku:2000*, May 2000

"20th Century Inspirations," *The Garden Design Journal*, Early Spring 2000

The Environment and Landscape Architecture of Korea, No. 5, 2000

"Exchange Rates," Chris Young, *Landlines*, February 2000

C3 Korea, No. 185, 2000

"Cement Gardens," Elspeth Thompson, *The Sunday Telegraph Magazine*, 9 January 2000

"Martha's Pop-Parks," Alexander Hosch, *Architectural Digest*, December/January 1999/2000

"The Davis Garden, El Paso, Texas," *Land Forum*, No. 3, 1999

"Jacob Javits Plaza in New York door Martha Schwartz," Linette Widder, *de Architect Dossiers*, November 1999

"Richiami Simbolici," Gilberto Oneto, *Ville Giardini*, October 1999

Gardens Illustrated, September 1999

"Martha Schwartz, Inc," *Landscape Architect and Specifier News*, September 1999

"Dance of the Drumlins," Paul Bennett, *Landscape Architecture*, August 1999

"Rus in Urbe," *The Architectural Review*, July 1999

"Bunte Pop-Art-Gärten," Katharina Sand, *Bolero*, June 1999

"Avant Garden," Liz Vannah, *Munich Found*, June 1999

"Fields of Fantasy," *Monument*, 29

"Bezüge zur Unter(wasser)welt," Thies Schröder, *Garten +Landschaft*, May 1999

"Zwei Plazas von Martha Schwartz," Gina Crandell, *Garten + Landschaft*, May 1999

"Breuer haha," *Wallpaper**, April 1999

"Public Art in Broward County: An Interview with Jean Grier," Stanley Collyer, *Competitions*, Spring 1999

"Il complesso residenziale di Kitagata, Gifu," Arata Isozaki, *Lotus 100*

"Mit Grünen Buckeln Gegen Langweile," *Haüser*, April 1999

"Sag mir, wo die Blumen sind," Claudia Voigt, *KulturSpiegel*, April 1999

"An Unconventional Artist," Chris Young, *Landscape Design*, March 1999

"An Interview with Martha Schwartz," Heidi Kost-Gross, *Perspectives in Landscape Design*, Winter 1999

"Remaking Manchester," Peter Neal, *Landscape Design*, September 1998

"Die Pop-Gärtnerin," Elke von Radziewsky, *Architektur & Wohnen*, January 1999

"Gardino Messicano," Ada Maria Ornaghi, *Abitare*, August 1998

"White Out," Bradford McKee, *Architecture*, August 1998

"Flying Saucers at HUD," Benjamin Forgey, *The Washington Post*, 6 June 1998

"The Battle for Pep-O-Mint Plaza," Bradford McKea, *Washington City Paper*, 22 May 1998

"Three Projects for Public Spaces in America," Dean Cardasis, *Domus*, March 1998

"Return to Spoleto," Eleanor Heartney, *Art in America*, December 1997

"Interview with Martha Schwartz and Jacques Simon," Quim Rosell, *2G*, No. 3, 1997

"The Grove as Pop Art: Martha Schwartz," Lynnette Widder, *Daidalos*, September 1997

"Miami Rhapsody," Michael Webb, *Metropolis*, September 1997

"Toward a New Living Environment: Gifu Kitagata Housing Project," *Space and Design*, August 1997

"On the Subject of Human Nature," Jane Brown Gillette, *Landscape Architecture*, August 1997

"Avant Gardener," Wendy Moonan, *House & Garden*, April 1997

"Self Portrait," Jane Brown Gillette, *Landscape Architecture*, February 1997

"Serra to Schwartz," Heidi Landecker, *Architecture*, January 1997

"Que Serra, Serra," Karrie Jacobs, *New York*, 20 January 1997

Innovative Design Solutions in Landscape Architecture, Steven L. Cantor, Van Nostrand Reinhold, New York, 1997

Martha Schwartz: Transfiguration of the Commonplace, Elizabeth K. Meyer, Spacemaker Press, Berkeley, 1997

Paradise Transformed: The Private Garden for the Twenty-First Century, Guy Cooper and Gordon Taylor, Monacelli Press, New York, 1996

"Natura e Artefatto," Isotta Cortesi, *AREA*, September/October 1996

Between Landscape Architecture and Land Art, Udo Weilacher, Birkhäuser, Basel and Boston, 1996

Ortho's Guide to Creative Home Landscaping, Ortho Books, San Ramon, 1996

"The Haunting of Federal Plaza," John Beardsley, *Landscape Architecture*, May 1996

"Miami Beach Comes of Age," Raul A. Barreneche, *Architecture*, April 1996

"Sculpting the Land," John Beardsley, *Sculpture*, Vol. 15, No. 4, 1996

"Imaginary Gardens With Real Frogs – Space in the Work of Martha Schwartz," Dean Cardasis, *GSD News*, Winter/Spring 1996

"Federal Buildings and Campuses," Vernon Mays, *Architecture*, January 1996

"Landschaftspark Messestadt Riem, Muenchen," *Wettbewerbe Aktuell*, Vol. 12, 1995

"Landschaftspark Muenchen-Riem," Horst Burger and Andrea Gebhard, *Garten + Landschaft*, December 1995

"Peter Walker und Martha Schwartz," Udo Weilacher, *Die Gartenkunst*, Vol. 7, No. 1, 1995

"Face to Face – Martha Schwartz, Inc," Graham Vickers, *World Architecture*, No. 36

"A Crab for Baltimore?" Andy Brown, *Landscape Architecture*, June 1994

"Tile, Style and Landscape Architecture," Carter Crawford, *Landscape Design*, April 1994

"A Contemporary Approach to the Ageless Vistas of Santa Fe," Verlyn Klinkenborg, *Architectural Digest*, December 1993

"Bass Museum Expansion," Projects Section, *Progressive Architecture*, November 1993

"Shaping a New American Landscape," Yoshiko Kasuga, *Pronto USA Magazine*, Vol. 10, No. 9, 1993

"Urban Outfitter," Myriam Weisang Misrach, *Elle*, September 1993

"Landscape & Common Culture Since Modernism," Martha Schwartz, *Architecture California*, Vol. 14, No. 2, November 1992

"Parc de la Citadelle," Martha Schwartz, *Pages Paysages*, Vol. 4, September 1992

Piscines, Sophie Roche-Soulie, Publications du Moniteur, September 1992

"On the Edge in Sante Fe," David Dillon, *Garden Design*, May/June 1992

"Our Culture and the Art for Public Places," Martha Schwartz, International IFLA Conference, *Artivisual Landscapes*, 1992

"Five Views: One Landscape, A Journal of Experiment in Public Art," Myra Mayman, Cathleen McCormick, Office for the Arts at Harvard & Radcliffe, 1992

"Freeway Landmark," Lynn Nesmith, *Architecture*, December 1991

"The Citadel Grand Allée, Honor Award," and "Becton Dickinson Atrium, Merit Award," *Landscape Architecture*, November 1991

"A Cross Cultural Concert in the Far East," Sally Woodbridge & Hiroshi Watanabe, *Progressive Architecture*, August 1991

"Perspectives: Landscape Architecture," Anne Whiston Spirn, Diana Balmori & Martha Schwartz, *Progressive Architecture*, August 1991

"Becton Dickinson," Monica Geran, *Interior Design*, August 1991

The Japan Architect, Vol. 5, 1991

"Landart," Elsa Leviseur, *The Architectural Review*, April 1991

Environmental Design: Architecture and Technology, Margaret Cottom-Winslow, PBC International, New York, 1991

"Martha Schwartz: Consumption Landscape," Marta Cervello, *Quaderns*, No. 185, April–June 1990

"Neue welle fürs Gartendesign," Horst Rasch, *Haüser*, No. 6, November 1990

"Von Künstlern entworfen: Gärten der Zukunft?" Elke von Radziewsky and Vera Graf, *Architektur & Wohnen*, No. 5, October/November 1990

"The Avant-Gardeners," Deborah Papier, *Avenue*, June/July 1990

"New American Landscapes," *Dialogue*, No. 4, 1990

"Portfolio: The 'New Wave' in Landscaping," Daralice D. Boles, *Trends*, Japan, No. 2, 1990

"Rhombus Room," Deborah Papier, and "A Convergence of 'Isms'," *Landscape Architecture*, January 1990

"Kashii District Housing, Architectural Design Citation," *Progressive Architecture*, 1990

"Rio Shopping Center, Merit Award" and "Turf Parterre, Merit Award," *Landscape Architecture*, November 1989

"The Innovators," *Newsweek*, 2 October, 1989

"The Rebirth of the Garden," Frances Anderton, *The Architectural Review*, September 1989

"Look Both Ways," Jim Murphy, *Progressive Architecture*, August 1989

"A Machine in the Forest," Vernon Mays, *Progressive Architecture*, August 1989

"P/A Profile, Peter Walker and Martha Schwartz," Daralice D. Boles, *Progressive Architecture*, July 1989

"Turf Parterre Garden," in *The New Urban Landscape*, Richard Martin (ed.), Olympia & York Companies, New York, 1989

"Martha Schwartz's 'Splice Garden': A Warning to a Brave New World," Jory Johnson, *Landscape Architecture*, July/August 1988

"American Landscape Architecture: Martha Schwartz," Toru Mitani, *SD Magazine*, Japan, August 1988

"Harmony in Design," Julie Bondurant, *Garden Design*, Summer 1988

"Transforming the American Garden," Jean Feinberg, *Landscape Architecture Magazine*, July 1986 (also reviewed by Patricia Phillips, *Art Forum Magazine*, September 1986)

Insights on Site: Perspectives on Art in Public Places, Stacy Paleologos Harris (ed.), Partners for Livable Places, Washington DC, 1985

"Planting Plastic," Paula Deitz, *The New York Times*, 22 September 1985

"Stella Schwartz Garden," Martha Schwartz, *Landscape Architecture*, May 1984

"M.I.T. May-Day Garden," Martha Schwartz, *Landscape Architecture*, May 1982

"Bagel Garden," *Landscape Architecture*, January 1980

Picture Credits

Art on File 148–51

Lena Ason 114–15, 220 [bottom center left]

Boora Architects 220 [bottom far right]

Boston Photo Image 74 [bottom left & center], 184, 190 [top left & bottom left], 209

Rick Casteel (computer illustrations) 34 [left], 52 [left column]

Lital Fabian 108–11, 156–57

Shauna Gillies-Smith 76

Tim Harvey 32–33, 34–35, 36, 37 [top left & bottom left], 38–41

George Heinrich 90, 91 [left & top right], 218 [bottom center right]

Jörg Hempel 198–205, 219 [bottom center left]

Markus Jatsch 144–45, 146 [center left, bottom left & right], 219 [top center left]

Paula Meijerink 116–17 [center], 154 [top left], 178 [right], 179 [top right], 180–81 [center], 181 [right], 218 [bottom center left]

David Meyer 66–67, 70 [left], 166–67, 168–69 [center], 217 [top far left]

Michael Moran 68–69, 70 [right], 71

Orlando Noa 104–5

Rion Rizzo/Creative Sources Atlanta 161 [bottom left & bottom right], 216 [top far right]

Lisa Roth 65 [top left & bottom left], 216 [bottom far right]

Martha Schwartz 37 [top right & bottom right], 44–45, 72–73, 74–75, 77 [top], 88–89, 91 [bottom right], 92–93, 96 [left], 97 [top], 98 [bottom left], 99, 100–3, 106–107, 116 [top left & bottom left], 117 [right], 118–19, 130–43, 146 [top left], 147, 152–53, 154 [right & bottom left], 155, 158-59, 160 [right], 161 [top], 162–65, 170–71, 174 [bottom left & bottom right], 176–77, 179 [left & bottom right], 180 [left], 185 [left & top right]], 186–87, 189, 190 [top right & bottom right], 191, 194–95, 196 [top row], 197 [top far left & bottom left], 216 [top center left], 217 [bottom center left], 218 [top center left, top center right & bottom far left], 219 [top far right & bottom far right], 220 [bottom far left]

Don Sharp 18–19, 48–49, 78–79, 182–83, 185 [bottom right], 219 [bottom far left]

Ken Smith 217 [top far right]

SS Nagoya Co. Ltd 128–29

Nic Tenwiggenhorn 192–93, 196 [bottom row],197 [top center left, top center right, top far right & bottom right]

Marc Treib 58–59, 60 [top], 61, 216 [bottom center right]

Jay Venezia 169 [top right & bottom right]

David Walker 54–57

Peter Walker 216 [top center right]

Robert Walker 62–63, 64 [right], 65 [bottom right]

Michael Wasser 74 [top right]

Alan Ward 2–3, 28–29, 31, 42–43, 46, 47, 51, 52–53, 94–95, 96–97 [center], 97 [bottom], 98 [top & bottom right], 172–73, 173 [center], 174 [top], 175, 185 [center right], 216 [top far left], 218 [bottom far right]

224